The Transforming
of a Tradition

The Transforming
of a Tradition

*Churches of Christ in
the New Millennium*

edited by
Leonard Allen & Lynn Anderson

NEW LEAF BOOKS / Orange, CA

THE TRANSFORMING OF A TRADITION
published by New Leaf Books

Copyright 2001 by C. Leonard Allen

ISBN 0-9700836-4-5
Printed in the United States of America

ALL RIGHTS RESERVED
No part of this publication may be reproduced, stored in a retrieval system, or transmitted in any form by any means—electronic, mechanical, photocopying, recording or otherwise—without prior written consent.

For information:
New Leaf Books, 12542 S. Fairmont, Orange, CA 92869
1-877-634-6004 (toll free)

02 03 04 05 06 07   9 8 7 6 5 4 3 2 1

In order to stay the same, a thing must change often.

—John Henry Newman

When you pass through the waters, I will be with you.

—Isaiah 43:2 (NIV)

The Christian pilgrim should pass from one age to another with the ease and serenity of freedom, assisting the new which is always struggling to be born, because in every age he loves not the times or some abstract truth but the neighbor.

—Paul Ramsey (1950)

Table of Contents

Contributors 9

Introduction
The Transforming of a Tradition *13*
C. Leonard Allen

Heritage
1. How Do You Spell Restoration? *25*
Tim Woodroof

2. "The Last Will and Testament of the Churches of Christ" *35*
Rob McRay

Church
3. Our Enduring Priesthood *49*
Linda King

4. The Challenge of Worship Renewal *63*
Randy Gill

5. The War is Over *75*
Milton Jones

6. Beyond the Quick Fix *85*
Phil Ware

7. Facing Our True Selves: Becoming Voices
of Courage in a New Era *93*
Paul Casner

Culture

8. A Final Farewell to the Twelfth Century *105*
Dale Pauls

9. Tradition: The Rural Church's
Vehicle for Change *117*
Rodger Weems

10. Mission Impossible? *129*
Chris Smith

Mission

11. The Church that Connects at Calvary *143*
Mark Love

12. A Place for the Lonely *157*
Kevin Wooten

13. Can an Institutional Church Become a
Missional Congregation? *175*
Grady King

14. A Plea for Passion *189*
Buddy Bell

Conclusion

A Dream Worth Keeping *199*
Lynn Anderson

Contributors

Lynn Anderson directs HopeNetwork, a ministry serving hundreds of ministers and church leaders around the country. He speaks frequently at churches, lectureships and seminars, and is the author of numerous books, including *Navigating the Winds of Change*, *They Smell Like Sheep: Spiritual Leadership for the 21st Century*, and *The Shepherd's Song: Finding the Heart to Go On*. He ministered with the Highland Church of Christ in Abilene, Texas, for 20 years; his passion now is encouraging and equipping ministers on the frontlines of congregational ministry. He and his wife Carolyn live in San Antonio, Texas.

Buddy Bell is the preaching minister for the Landmark Church of Christ in his hometown of Montgomery, Alabama. He previously ministered with churches in Tuscaloosa, Alabama and Pensacola, Florida. He holds degrees from the University of Alabama (B.A.) and Southern Christian University (M.A., Bible). He has extensive experience and success in small group ministry, and speaks frequently at revivals, retreats and lectureships. He is married to the former Stephanie Beasley and they have four children, Laura, Lindsey, Luke and Lincoln.

Paul Casner grew up on a farm in southern Indiana. He holds degrees from David Lipscomb University (B.A.), Abilene Christian University (M.A., M.Div.) and Marquette University (Ph.D., theology). Over the years he has ministered to Churches of Christ in Indiana, Texas and New York. Paul and his wife Nancy have been married 15 years and have one daughter.

Randy Gill is the Worship Minister for the Woodmont Hills Church of Christ in Nashville, Tennessee. Previously he was Associate Director of Church Relations and a professor at Pepperdine University. He has also served on the faculties of Rochester College and Oklahoma Christian University. In addition to his activities as a worship leader, teacher and musician, Randy is a popular speaker at churches, youth rallies and retreats. His video series "That's

Entertainment?" has been used by youth groups across the country. Randy has degrees from Rochester College, Harding University, University of Michigan, and the University of Southern California. He is married to LaJuana Case Gill and they have a 20-year-old son named Christopher.

Milton Jones has ministered with the Northwest Church of Christ in Seattle, Washington for the past 25 years. Prior to that he worked with the Broadway Church in Lubbock ministering on the campus of Texas Tech. He holds degrees from Texas Tech (B.B.A.), Eastern New Mexico University (M.A., Religion), and California Graduate School of Theology (D.Min.). and serves as an adjunct professor at Pugent Sound Christian College. He is the author of *Discipling: The Multiplying Ministry*, *Grace: The Heart of the Fire*, and, most recently, *Christ—No More, No Less: How to be a Christian in a Postmodern World*. He and his wife Barbi are the parents of two sons, Patrick and Jeremy.

Grady D. King preaches for the South MacArthur Church of Christ, Irving, Texas. He and his wife, Karen have two children, Josh (17) and Christin (13). Grady is a graduate of Oklahoma Christian University (B.S. Education, 1977) and Abilene Christian University (M.S. Biblical and Related Studies, 1989) and is presently working toward a Master of Divinity. He has served as youth minister and preacher for rural, suburban and urban congregations in Oklahoma (McAlester, Muskogee) and Texas (Grand Prairie, Austin, Mansfield). He is most passionate about the church being community-oriented, multi-cultural and, most of all, redemptive.

Linda King holds degrees from Oklahoma Christian College (B.A.) and the University of Oklahoma (J.D.). She and husband Eric King live in Edmond, Oklahoma, and have practiced law together for almost 25 years. They are the parents of three grown children and the proud grandparents of four grandsons. In 1982 Linda and Eric helped begin Dayspring Church of Christ, where she currently serves as chair of the Adult Education Committee. In 1994 she helped found U R Special Ministries, Inc., a charitable corporation which provides new back-to-school, Christmas and Easter outfits for 500 needy and at-risk children each year.

Mark Love, at the time this essay was written, was minister of the word for the East County Church of Christ in Gresham, Oregon. He served in that capacity from 1990 through July 2001. Mark currently serves as Director of Ministry Events at Abilene Christian University, where he directs the annual lectureship and teaches courses on ministry. He is the author of *Matthew: Finding Treasure New and Old* (2000), and has written articles for *Leaven*, *Wineskins* and other publications. Mark and his wife Nancy (McLeskey) have one son, Joshua.

Rob McRay has served as the preaching minister for the Bering Drive Church of Christ in Houston, Texas, since 1997. Before that he served ten years at the Northtown Church in Milwaukee, Wisconsin, and has been a minister since 1980. Rob is a graduate of Abilene Christian University (B.A., Bible) and Wheaton College (M.A., Biblical Studies). He has written articles for *Leaven, Integrity, 21st Century Christian* and *Wineskins*. His wife Judy is a registered nurse, and they have a daughter at Abilene Christian and a son in high school.

Dale Pauls has ministered with the Stamford Church of Christ in Stamford, Connecticut for the past 23 years. As a supplement to ministry he has devoted considerable time to graduate studies in Medieval History at New York University. One of his special interests is tracing how attitudes to church, law and spirituality that were shaped in twelfth-century Europe have continued to influence churches today. He holds degrees from Harding University (B.A.), Harding Graduate School of Religion (M.A., M.Th.), and New York University (M.Phil.). He also serves on the board of Camp Shiloh, an outreach program to inner-city children in the greater New York City area.

Chris Smith serves as pulpit minister for the Harpeth Hills Church of Christ in Brentwood, Tennessee. He previously served churches in Tennessee, Kentucky and Texas. He graduated from David Lipscomb University (B.A.) and Harding Graduate School of Religion (M.Th.). Chris speaks frequently at brotherhood events and has published many articles in magazines and journals. He and his wife Vicki have been married 20 years and have three children.

Phil Ware has ministered with the Westover Hills Church of Christ in Austin, Texas, for the past 19 years. Over the years Phil has spoken at seminars, lectureships, retreats and campus outreach events, and written articles for several publications. He holds degrees from Abilene Christian University (B.A., M.A.). He serves as president of Heartlight, Inc., a web-based ministry located at www.Heartlight.org. Heartlight reaches over 240,000 distinct users each month off the web site and sends out 100,000 devotionals per day to people all over the world. He and his wife are the parents of two children, Zach and Megan.

Rodger Weems began preaching regularly at age 16, while still in high school. He graduated from Temple College (A.A.), the University of Mary Hardin-Baylor (B.A., English and Speech), and Abilene Christian University (M.S., Bible). He has spoken at the ACU Lectureship and other programs. His most recent ministry was a ten-year tenure with the Graham Street Church of Christ in Stephenville, Texas.

Tim Woodroof ministers with the Otter Creek Church of Christ in Nashville, Tennessee. Previously he and his wife Julie served churches in Lincoln, Nebraska, and Beaverton, Oregon. Tim holds degrees from Harding University (B.S.), Texas A & M University (M.S.), and the University of Nebraska (Ph.D.). He is the author of *Walk This Way*, *A Church That Flies: A New Call to Restoration in Churches of Christ*, and *A Distant Presence* (a work of historical fiction based on the church at Philippi forthcoming from NavPress in late 2001). Tim enjoys reading, being a father, and fly fishing. In their spare time, Tim and Julie publish educational material for churches (www.lookpress.com).

Kevin Wooten and his life-partner, Mary, have worked together on the University of Kentucky campus for 11 years. They have a 10-year-old son, Zack, and a 7-year-old daughter, Jenna. Every free warm day you will find this family at a lake enjoying the water. Most other free moments you may find Kevin and Mary putting a few more miles on their running shoes. The spark for this family was first ignited in a campus ministry at Western Kentucky University. Nearly 15 years later the flame is still alive. Kevin went from WKU to Abilene Christian University for a graduate degree, then to Vero Beach, Florida to preach. Lexington is their home now and campus ministry remains their passion.

Introduction

The Transforming of a Tradition

Leonard Allen

Tidal Waves

In a provocative new book, Leonard Sweet writes: "The seismic events that have happened in the aftermath of the postmodern earthquake have generated tidal waves that have created a whole new world out there. In your lifetime and mine a tidal wave has hit....The Dick-and-Jane world of my '50s childhood is over, washed away by a tsunami of change. [Electronic technologies have] created a sea change such as the world has never experienced before, including a huge shift in religious sensibility."[1]

Sweet says that churches can respond to this tidal wave in one of three ways. First, they can deny it—and drown. This response has left a lot of churches only "a couple of funerals away from closing." Second, they can fight it—and lose. They see the tidal wave coming and choose to hunker-in-the-bunker; but there is no safe bunker in which to hunker. Third, they can hoist the sails, catch God's wave and make some waves themselves. They can recognize the enormous opportunities this new era presents and attempt to seize them.

Even if Sweet's estimation of the magnitude of the wave of change is only half right, Christians are in for a terrific dousing.

Leonard Allen

A Critical Time for Churches of Christ

Clearly Churches of Christ are in a critical time. The glory days—the post-World War II years when the ranks of Churches of Christ were swelling, when vigorous debates with denominationalists were still the order of the day, and when the message of the One True Church was unambiguous and powerful—have passed, and many members feel troubled and fearful, perhaps guilty and certainly disoriented. Many congregations are stuck, either settled into a defensive holding pattern or wracked by the tensions of younger families pressing for change and renewal. Some leaders mount vigorous polemical campaigns to sound the alarm; others of a gentler, less combative nature quietly grieve what they believe to be the apostasy of those who break with the traditional doctrinal system. The language of "going off" to the denominations, long part of the vocabulary of Churches of Christ, still sounds frequently in the ranks (at least in some parts of the country), though it is becoming more and more a whisper instead of a shout.

One recent polemicist asserts, for example, that Churches of Christ are undergoing a "quiet revolution" and that few seem properly concerned. Caught up in a "frenzy of ecumenical fervor," he argues, Churches of Christ are presently experiencing a "radical abandonment of settled doctrine." The Protestant "faith only" doctrine is replacing the historic insistence on the essentiality of baptism, with the result that their "exclusive circle of fellowship" is breaking down. As a result Churches of Christ are facing a sharp and troubling crisis of identity.[2] Whatever one may think of this polemicist's prescription, his analysis seems basically correct.

Churches of Christ became a sizable and dynamic Christian movement in twentieth-century America. Their appeal was the claim to have restored the True Church which had been corrupted and lost by human denominational traditions. Many thousands of Baptists, Methodists, Presbyterians, Lutherans, Catholics, Pentecostals and believers from sundry other Christian churches were taught that they were not True Christians and converted to the True Church. Indeed, most of the evangelistic literature of twentieth-century Churches of Christ, until recently, focused on such conversions. It was standard practice—and remains so among traditionalists—to speak of a Baptist, a Pentecostal or a Catholic becoming a "New Testament Christian" and a member of the "Lord's Church."[3] These claims and practices were integral to the tradition; a whole doctrinal system undergirded them. This system remains intact for many members, and popular polemicists continue to defend and promote it aggressively. Yet among many others this system has receded or even been rejected. Without this system in place, it is unclear who or what Churches of Christ will be. Without it they will have to forge a new identity—an arduous and stressful undertaking.

Up until a decade or two ago almost every congregation of Churches of Christ had on display somewhere in its building the tract entitled "Neither Catholic, Protestant, nor Jew"—or one like it. People commonly "classify the church of Christ," said the tract, "as just another denomination of the Protestant group. We would like to convey to them that the category does not fit." Though we "may possess some of the characteristics of Catholics, Protestants, and Jews," it insisted, "we are not members of any ecclesiastical group. We are just Christians only, members of Christ's church."[4] This claim was fundamental to how Churches of Christ understood themselves; indeed such a claim helped form the identity of the movement from its inception.

Undergirding this basic claim was the language of "restoration." From their modern inception Churches of Christ have been a "restoration movement." They called people to a fresh restoration of, not Protestant, not Catholic, but New Testament Christianity. That call has been at the heart of their identity. But now many church members, especially among the younger generations, are wondering about restoration—about the concept, the very word itself. Many are coming to feel that Churches of Christ have over-reached themselves, majored in minors, been too hard and exclusive and perhaps even discredited the very term "restoration." More and more people seem, for whatever reason, to be quietly dropping the language of restoration. For these church members the implicit questions—only occasionally made explicit—seem to be: Do we really want to be a restoration movement today? Is the traditional language still serviceable? Do we really want to remain where that rhetoric has brought us and to own the identity it has given us?

Nothing has been more central and distinctive to the identity of Churches of Christ in the last century than the practice of worshipping without instrumental music. Far from a mere preference or guiding principle, it was a strict prohibition based on an interpretive method that viewed everything not commanded or exampled in the New Testament as forbidden. Instrumental music was, in short, a sin, an act of rebellion against God's design for true worship. A cappella worship became one of the most distinctive features of Churches of Christ and thus a central element in its ethos and identity.[5]

Striking examples of the proportions that this issue has assumed are the following two statements, both published recently in a leading, mainstream church magazine: "the introduction and use of mechanical instruments of music into Christian worship," wrote an influential Bible commentator and preacher, "is sinful and is perhaps the most sinful thing that any true church of our Lord could do in this generation." Another well-known preacher said that "instrumental music only lets the cat out of the bag….After they bring in the instrument, baptism is no longer essential, and the church is just another denomination among denominations."[6]

Traditionalists believe that instrumental music in worship is sinful and puts one out of fellowship with God, though sometimes they hold this view less polemically and more quietly. Almost no progressive leaders believe instrumental worship to be sinful, though many believe it would be divisive (and thus sinful) to embrace or impose it at present. Beyond this shift, the progressives continue the practice of a cappella worship for various reasons: some believe it best because it reflects the practice of the primitive churches; a good many prefer it because they grew up with it; some think it a good safeguard against the transformation of worship into entertainment; some put a new spin on the tradition by saying that there should be a place for a cappella churches within the larger Christian world; and some simply accommodate the practice as a political necessity.

All of these reasons may be good rationales for continuing the traditional practice; but all of them are departures from the rationale of the core tradition, and will not satisfy many traditionalists—indeed, such reasons will probably not be strong enough to maintain the tradition widely among progressive churches in the long run. In this music-saturated culture and with a generation of Christian young people—not to mention the unchurched—who can embrace the traditional practice only with an arduous leap, the force of mere preference and accommodation will not carry the tradition forward for long. Most of the traditionalists and some of the progressives know this.

Certainly these are changing, unnerving times. In our culture and in our churches anchors are pulling away, things are coming loose. That much, at least, should be overwhelmingly clear to just about everyone.

A Modern Church after the Modern Age

We are entering a post-denominational age. Denominational loyalties are markedly receding and the old denominational map is becoming less useful to navigate the American Christian terrain. As George Marsden put it, once people have discovered that all brands of gasoline are basically the same, what they look for is octane. So with denominationalism. For more and more people, spiritual power and vitality is what they seek, not so much a particular brand of church. And they will find it where they can. Further, new, "back-to-the-Bible" churches claiming to be non-denominational are springing up like mushrooms, making claims that sound a lot like the early Churches of Christ. Indeed, we are entering a period some are referring to as a "new reformation," a period when traditional Protestant visions of church life, organization and ministry are being fundamentally challenged and rethought.[7]

At one level, the transformations being wrought on Churches of Christ can be viewed as the old "sect to denomination" process proceeding like clockwork (as H. R. Niebuhr described in general and as David Edwin Harrell has documented extensively in the Stone-Campbell tradition).[8] This transformation is both a sociological process (moving from less affluent and respectable to more affluent and respectable) and a theological process (moving from harder, narrower claims to softer, wider ones). Among Churches of Christ, this shift has been underway since at least the 1960s but is only now becoming widely visible. Only now are younger people who have already made this shift widely coming into positions of power in the congregations and schools.

At another, more profound (and more interesting) level, the transformations in Churches of Christ are being wrought by a momentous worldview shift. For good or for ill—probably for both—the world of the modern is receding and a new era is emerging. We are now in a time of dramatic worldview change. The modern worldview, with its built-in secular biases and boundless confidence that humans could manage, unite and control the world, is being dislodged. Some say it has crumbled.

As I have shown in my earlier work, the character of Churches of Christ, despite the pervasive restorationist claims, has been profoundly (early) modern.[9] Churches of Christ, along with many other ardent moderns, thus find themselves in a serious bind: they are a distinctly (early) modern church entering a postmodern world. Here at the beginning of the new millennium, that fact, more than any other, accounts for the swift and disorienting changes they are experiencing. Indeed, the changes underway are more profound and sweeping than those most worried about change seem yet to realize.

The good news is that God appears to be working in powerful and fresh ways at this juncture in history. Some of the old polarizations are breaking up and old alienating labels are becoming less functional. There is an opening, a ripeness, that seems to arise in the shake-up and disorientation that comes with the passing of one era and the emergence of another. A change of eras certainly brings new (or at least redesigned) pitfalls, but it also tends to wake the sleeping, unsettle the settled, prod the smug, anger or alarm the doctrinaire, and do numerous other good things for bored or complacent Christians. These are not safe and settled times, but they are—or should be—adventurous and exciting times. And as Stanley Hauerwas has reminded us, "God has not promised us safety, but participation in an adventure called the Kingdom. That seems to me to be great news in a world that is literally dying of boredom."[10]

As several writers in this volume indicate, Churches of Christ, along with the other Christian traditions, are being forced more and more to face up to the realities of becoming missionaries in their own culture and of forming missionary congregations. And missionary congregations in our chaotic postmodern culture will look and function differently from the churches of "Christian America" that we have grown accustomed to. Indeed, the new cultural status of Christians calls for "a new, post-Christendom definition of the church."[11]

As for the "quiet revolution" that so troubles traditionalists, not all the change stirring and troubling Churches of Christ today is due to secularism, biblical illiteracy or cultural sellout, as the polemicists seem to think. Some of it is, of course. But some of it is a fitful critique of and move away from earlier (nineteenth-century) cultural accommodation by the tradition itself. Alexander Campbell's theological system was a critical response to early nineteenth-century revivalism and an effective accommodation of the new spirit of individualism and liberty set loose in America. But his theology was deeply shaped by the culture of that time, including the bold conviction that one could stand free of culture and tradition and "just read the Bible." David Lipcomb's theological stance was deeply formative for Churches of Christ, as it combined Campbell's interpretive principles with a counter-cultural apocalypticism. But his theology was deeply shaped, to cite just one example, by the culture of "true womanhood" dominant in mid-nineteenth-century America.[12] We do not have the option of choosing between a cultural church or a non-cultural church; culture is the unavoidable medium of the church's life. It has always been a "cultural church," and some of the present ferment has come as people have realized that nineteenth-century enculturation and accommodation was not eternal and in some respects no longer healthy or appropriate.

The Basic Questions

The questions before the writers in this collection of essays are not, Are Churches of Christ changing? and, Will they continue to change to better fit this new era as it unfolds? (They are. And they will.) Rather, the questions are, How will Churches of Christ deal with the profound sea-changes that are well underway and yet remain dynamic and faithful in their mission to the glory of God? And, How can they do this in a way that maintains some kind of meaningful continuity with their past?

The essayists chosen for this collection are younger leaders who are coming into their time and whose primary ministry is with churches, not colleges or universities. The essays reflect what concerns them most, what challenges them most, what excites them most as Churches of Christ cross the threshold of a new millennium and seek to minister to a culture that seems lightyears away from the rural world in which they took shape and first flourished.

These essayists are not simply advocates for the transforming of Churches of Christ; they are also themselves reflections of a transformation already well under way. One can read their work as thoughtful, creative, often passionate analysis of trends and challenges among present Churches of Christ—work that will stimulate, provoke and encourage other leaders. But one can also read it as a window into how a new generation of leaders has already been transformed—and how, as a result, they construe their heritage and their future in new ways.

Tidal waves are upon us. In the midst of the dousing, these leaders—all of them in the thick of congregational leadership—are seeking to hoist the sails and catch the strong breezes. They are trying to see with clear eyes the enormous new opportunities around us, and to seize them for the furtherance of God's Kingdom.

Notes

1. Leonard I. Sweet, *SoulTsunami: Sink or Swim in New Millennium Culture* (Grand Rapids: Zondervan, 1999). For a different, more critical and challenging view of this new cultural era, see Tom Sine, *Mustard Seed versus McWorld: Reinventing Life and Faith for the Future* (Grand Rapids, MI: Baker, 1999).

2. LaGard Smith, *Who Is My Brother? Facing a Crisis of Identity and Fellowship* (Malibu, CA: Cotswold, 1997).

3. For my limited purposes in this chapter I use the simple categories of

"progressive" and "traditionalist" to describe basic forces presently at work in Churches of Christ. For an attempt at a more complex taxonomy of the present "camps" and tensions, see Douglas Foster, *Will the Cycle Be Unbroken?: Churches of Christ Face the Twenty-First Century* (Abilene, TX: ACU, 1994), 89-98.

4. Batsell Baxter and Carroll Ellis, "Neither Catholic, Protestant, nor Jew" (Nashville, TN: Hillsboro Church of Christ, n.d.), 5, 6. These claims are ubiquitous in the literature of Churches of Christ.

5. Among the vast polemical literature on this subject, see for example these recent and representative articles: Guy N. Woods, "Why Churches of Christ Do Not Use Instrumental Music in Worship," *Spiritual Sword* 24 (April 1993), 17-24; Hugo McCord, "Is Instrumental Music a Matter of Indifference?" *Spiritual Sword* 26 (April 1995), 33-34; J. W. Roberts, "Instrumental Music Is Unauthorized and Unprecedented," *Gospel Advocate* 134 (May 1992), 38-43; Bruce Harris, "Instrumental Music in Worship Is Sinful," *Firm Foundation* 102 (August 27, 1985), 511; and Jimmy Jividen, "Instrumental Music: A Point of Controversy," *Gospel Advocate* 138 (January 1996), 22-24.

6. Burton Coffman, "The Sinful Use of Instrumental Music," *Gospel Advocate* 137 (October 1995), 22; Charles Hodge, "Facing the Instrumental Music Question Again," ibid. 140 (February 1998), 24. Hodge concluded: "How important is the instrumental music issue? The entire future of our movement is at stake. May God have mercy upon us" (25).

7. See Greg Ogden, *The New Reformation: Returning the Ministry to the People of God* (Grand Rapids, MI: Zondervan, 1990); Donald E. Miller, "The New Face of American Protestantism: A Second Reformation?" *Reinventing American Protestantism: Christianity in the New Millennium* (Berkeley, CA: University of California, 1997), 11-26; Rodney Clapp, *A Peculiar People: The Church as Culture in a Post-Christian Society* (Downer's Grove, IL: InterVarsity, 1996); and Eddie Gibbs, *ChurchNext: Quantum Changes in How We Do Ministry* (Downer's Grove, IL: InterVarsity, 1999).

8. H. Richard Niebuhr, *The Social Sources of Denominationalism* (New York: World Publishing Co., 1972); David Edwin Harrell, "The Emergence of the Church of Christ Denomination" (booklet, 1966), and *The Churches of Christ in the Twentieth Century: Homer Hailey's Personal Journey of Faith* (Tuscaloosa, AL: University of Alabama, 2000).

9. See especially *The Cruciform Church: Becoming a Cross-Shaped People in a Secular World* (Abilene, TX: ACU, 1990), 19-38.

10. Stanley Hauerwas, "Preaching as Though We Had Enemies," *First Things* (May 1995), 48.

11. Craig Van Gelder, "A Great New Fact of Our Day: America as Mission Field," in *Between Gospel and Culture* (Grand Rapids: Eerdmans, 1997), 57-68.

12. See Fred Bailey, "Disciple Images of Victorian Womanhood," *Discipliana* 40 (Spring 1980), 7-12, and C. Leonard Allen, "Silena M. Holman (1850-1915), Voice of the 'New Woman' among Churches of Christ," ibid 56 (Spring 1996), 3-11.

──────────────── Heritage

1

How Do You Spell Restoration?

Tim Woodroof

Oliver Sachs, in the title piece from his wonderful book *The Man Who Mistook His Wife for a Hat*, tells of one of his neurological patients—Dr. P. This older gentleman—an accomplished musician, cultured and educated—developed a tumor in the visual cortex, resulting in strange but subtle problems. Dr. P. could dress himself, eat and carry on a conversation—until interrupted or distracted. Once the flow of his activity was broken, however, Dr. P. would freeze, motionless, staring unblinking into space. Having lost the thread of what he was about, Dr. P. came to a complete stop, forgetting himself and his surroundings. Only through gentle reminders of what he was doing and why could Dr. P. be persuaded to resume his activity.[1]

Movements, like people, can forget themselves. Interrupted or distracted, they can lose the thread that holds their activities together and gives them coherence. One moment we are marching along with a sense of purpose and identity. The next we are sitting paralyzed on the ground, wondering how we got here and where we are going. Something breaks into the flow of our activity and we find, to our surprise, that we can no longer recall what it was we were attempting to do.

The Churches of Christ are in such a period today. Somewhere along the way we have forgotten what we were doing and why. We find ourselves confused over the most basic questions: Who are we? and, What is our purpose? We've lost the thread that gives meaning to our activities, and, having done so, many of us have lost the motivation to continue doing what we no longer understand. We find ourselves paralyzed, not because we are too tired to go on, but because we despair of our activity resulting in something that God values.

The purposes we can articulate for the church—borrowed as they are from a prior generation and a radically different world—seem narrow and rote. In quiet and reflective moments, we question whether those goals are worthy of the sacrifices required. Many of us are no longer willing to pour the best of ourselves into the preservation of nineteenth-century modes of worship or doctrinal positions that—in our hearts—we no longer accept or believe to be central. Jesus did not die, nor do we want to live, to ensure that buildings not have kitchens or that music remain congregational and a cappella or that a woman never make announcements in church.

The debate over such matters is exhausting precisely because it seems so irrelevant. The world around us is sick and demented. Daily, we watch people being butchered and starved and exploited. Children are growing up fatherless. The greed of nations is devouring entire populations in mindless wars. "Sexual ethics" is oxymoronic and increasingly anachronistic. Politicians are corrupt; priests are perverse; and "there is violence in the land." It will take something more potent than correct positions on worship etiquette to make a dint in this present darkness.

And we know it.

Yet, from some memory older than the restoration plea or even than Christianity itself, comes the notion that the people of God should make a difference, a difference felt at the foundations of our culture. Whatever our purpose and mission, we know that it should be no little thing concerned with the fringes of life. If something is to break into our paralysis and startle us once more into activity, we must find a mission that is worthy of renewed efforts.

How Do You Spell Restoration?

In order for Churches of Christ to march into the third millennium with vigor, a recovery of purpose is required. Our fellowship, in short, needs to know that it is still on a mission from God. An effective, functioning, faithful church—a church that makes a difference, a church whose priorities and purposes serve the kingdom of God—that church must understand who it is, where it is going, what it values and why it exists.

For decades the notion that we were a "restoration people," called to "do Bible things in Bible ways," provided that sense of mission. We prided ourselves on replicating in modern times the ancient and primitive rites of first-century faith and practice. We were consumed with the identification and cataloguing of the early churches' modes of worship, examples of outreach and cooperation, their structures for leadership, the names by which they called themselves, the ethical standards by which they lived, and the means by which they expressed and maintained community. We believed that by becoming students of the early church and by adopting those ancient patterns of life for ourselves, we could restore the ancient church in modern times.

The duplication of the manner in which the earliest Christians "did church" became for many of us the central tenet of restoration efforts. The result of all those years of study and discussion was a real (if informal) consensus about how the first-century church acted and how, therefore, we ought to act. Did they take the supper every first day of the week? That pattern was seen as binding on any church that would be faithful today. Did they have five acts of worship? So must we, and neither less nor more. Did they have elders and deacons chosen on the pattern of 1 Timothy 3 and Titus 1? We must also have both elders and deacons (never one without the other), and those must be chosen strictly by the standards set out in the pastoral epistles. Did they have love feasts and greet each other with a holy kiss and speak in tongues during their worship services? Well, you can't take restoration too far!

But, of course, we did. Having gotten the restoration bit between our teeth, it was hard to know where to stop. How many cups did early Christians use for the supper? Was the bread they used one loaf or bite-sized pieces? Where was the biblical authority for a Sunday School or cooperative support for children's homes or a Missionary Society? Did early churches build church buildings or hire located ministers? Was it proper to erect family life centers and hold marriage seminars and feed hungry people who wouldn't sit still for a Bible lesson?

It was precisely over such questions that Churches of Christ have, for the past hundred years, reasoned and debated and argued. Eventually it was over such questions that we alienated and divided. To the outside observer, all this frenzy about ancient patterns and modern practice seems obtuse and even absurd. What such an observer would fail to understand is the critical assumption we were making even as we split over these theological hairs.

The assumption, rooted in no less a figure than Alexander Campbell, was that if we could replicate the ancient church in modern times the millennium would be ushered in. For Campbell, restoration was no mere tool for getting the church back on track. It would open the door for the return of Christ and the judgment of the world.[2] If only the first-century church could be resurrected, if only all people of good character would join together in practicing simple, primitive Christianity stripped of the accumulated theological baggage of the centuries, the path would be cleared for the promises of God to be fulfilled in toto.

Function Follows Form?

Of course, that was Campbell's assumption, not ours. As good amillennialists, we could not swallow Campbell's theories about the end times. But we could (and did) modify his assumption to one with which we were more comfortable. Why was it so important to conform our practice of church to the patterns and forms of the first-century? Because when we perfectly restored the first-century pattern, we believed we would usher in a revival of first-century power and effectiveness. Function would follow form. We convinced ourselves that the power, harmony, fervor and holiness we saw in the ancient church would break out afresh in the modern church—if only we could reinstate the pattern they followed. By "doing church" in the same way the ancients "did church," we too could become a church that turned the world upside down, changed lives and brought glory to God.

That was the assumption behind our perplexing obsession with the details of first-century church life. We did not study the past because we liked it better than the present. We scoured the past because we saw it as our best hope for functioning effectively in the here-and-now. Copy the modes of early worship and true worship would break out among us. Imitate the methods of early evangelism and the world (or at least the interested) would beat a path to our door. Model our leadership structure and styles after those found in Jerusalem or Antioch or Ephesus and God would bless us with leaders who were leaders indeed.

So captivated were we by this assumption regarding restoration that we took matters a step further. Not only would the pursuit of form lead us to function, but only the pursuit of form would do so. Only by discovering and reproducing the modes, methods and practices of the first-century church could we have any assurance that the resulting church would produce the fruit God wanted. There could be no legitimate leadership in the church, no trustable vision and divinely sanctioned authority, unless such leadership grew out of the New Testament pattern of elders, deacons and evangelists. There could be no legitimate worship, no true praise or pleasing sacrifice, unless that worship matched exactly in form and expression the patterns seen in the early church. There could be no legitimate evangelism unless, first and foremost, the means, methods and message used by the modern evangelist conformed precisely to the express or necessarily implied example of his ancient counterpart.

Unless the form was correct, the results didn't count.

Thus we found an ingenious way to kill two birds with one Bible. What is our mission? We are the ones who have discovered the key to revival for the church. Because we worship like the first churches and organize ourselves like them and adhere strictly to their ethic and do not practice any unauthorized "innovations," God is using us to rebuild in these last days a church through which he can freely work.

And what about all those other churches out there? Well, sadly, the good that they do is tainted because they are not doing it in the right way. Certainly, there are churches that have a powerful ministry of compassion for the poor, but because they are encumbered with a denominational structure, God will not bless their efforts or use them to expand his kingdom. And, yes, there are groups that have stressed the deepening of the spiritual life through prayer and confession; but they are unsound on the instrumental music question, so their spiritual wisdom is suspect. And there are examples in the religious world around us of harmonious fellowship, holy living, sincere worship, sacrificial generosity and dedicated service. All that is wasted on the kingdom, however. Because they fall short on the means, the ends cannot be valid.

Inspecting Our Fruit

All of which might be quite defensible if we could point to the results of our own efforts and show that, in fact, function has followed form for us. If the Churches of Christ could demonstrate that our key does indeed fit the lock for effective churches, that after 150 years of pursuing proper form we were finally functioning as the loving, holy, evangelistically fervent, compassionate, worshipful body of Christ envisioned by the apostles, there might be room for boasting about ourselves and discounting the efforts of others.

So what has been our fruit? I take nothing away from the good done in our fellowship over the years: the souls that have been won, the lives that have been changed, the sacrifices that have been made, the worship that has been offered. Yet enough time has passed, enough effort has been invested to allow the question, "Are we now functioning as the glorious church we want so badly to be?"

Has our obsession with New Testament patterns and duly authorized forms resulted in a more loving and united community? Having struggled so long with issues of church leadership, do we now provide a vivid and compelling model of strong, faithful, visionary leadership for the religious world around us? After all the dust has settled from our arguments over modes of baptism and issues surrounding discipleship, are we turning the world upside down with our passion to save the lost?

How Do You Spell Restoration?

Forced to admit that our movement has, in fact, stagnated, that we have divided ourselves into exhaustion, that we have not enjoyed the expected period of explosive growth, that our young people are leaving (or at least have discovered little passion for the vision which captured their fathers), that our worship periods have settled into a stultifying sameness, that our congregations are graying at a rapid rate or dying off entirely, a strange kind of rear-guard action is taking place in many quarters. Unwilling to accept that our assumptions about restoration may have been wrong, we are scrambling to find ways to shift the blame. It is not our efforts that have been misdirected, it is the times in which we live! We console ourselves with memories of Jeremiah's lonely ministry and Jesus' inability to perform miracles in Nazareth because of the people's "lack of faith." We tell ourselves that it is hard to be right, and quote like a mantra "narrow the road that leads to life, and only a few find it." Our present struggles have become almost a badge of honor, proving in a perverse way that we are on the right path—it's just that nobody is interested in the truth any more.

The prescription for the church advocated by those who take this tack is for the church to hunker down, protect it's gains, remain "faithful" especially in these difficult days—and (God help us) do more, much more, of the same thing we have been doing. If only we hang on, God will eventually bring the blessing we have all been taught to expect.

The Loyal Opposition

Not everyone, however, is taking that line. Some of us, reviewing the state of Churches of Christ at the dawn of the twenty-first century, are recognizing that drastic surgery is in order or else the patient may well expire on the table. To do more of the same will result in more of the same, and that we cannot afford. It is time to do something different so that we can make a difference.

These voices calling for change will not let our movement take refuge by circling the wagons against a hostile world. They refuse to shift the blame to a hardhearted culture or an increasingly unfaithful church. They remind us that if first-century Christians had heard Jesus' words about the "narrow road" in the same way we seem to be hearing them, there would have been no evangelistic push out of Jerusalem, no turning the world upside down. They still have faith that the Churches of Christ can find a way to function effectively in these dark times. As a consequence, they are far more willing to call into question the assumptions our movement has made about restoration and to wonder whether there might be another way to "do church" today than focusing on and imitating New Testament forms.

For a new generation in our churches (and for many in the older generation, I quickly and gratefully acknowledge), a critical decision has been made—function comes first, not form. These people yearn to be a Christ-like, Spirit-led, sanctified, disciple-making community that makes a difference in the world. For them, the only kind of restoration worth pursuing has little to do with resuscitating ancient methods and much to do with recapturing an ancient vision of who God's people are and what business they are to be about. They no longer believe that a restoration of proper forms will ensure proper functioning in the church. That belief has been beaten out of them by too many years of experience with churches consumed with forms and oblivious to the essential functions of God's people. They are convinced, instead, that it is those "essential functions" that must consume our attention.

Ask them if they are interested in restoring the first-century church and they will answer, "Yes!" But ask them what about the first-century church they want to restore, and you will hear things like "Their passionate worship," "Their effective outreach," or "Their sense of community." Restoration, for this generation, isn't about how the first-century church did business. It's about what business that church did. They would say that we should be focusing on core values, not tinkering with matters that are peripheral and tiny. "Form follows function," they will insist. "Get the functions right and God will provide the forms we need to do His business effectively."

And they want to be biblical. Only being "biblical" means paying attention to the "weightier matters of the law" rather than being tyrannized by the details. They have seen too many people in the Bible and in the modern church who have focused on twigs and missed the forest. They realize that "correctness" is not the same as "godliness," that doing things right is not synonymous with doing the right things. Being biblical, for them, means pursuing the same ends as the apostles and the first-century church, not using the same methods or adopting the same forms.

In fact, they confront us with a most difficult question. "Who is being more biblical? Who is really being faithful? The church that adopts innovative and creative methods of building a strong sense of community among its members or the church that is so wedded to particular forms it cannot effectively build loving relationships? The church that encourages a personal encounter with God through music, drama, testimonial and dialogue, or the church that sticks to traditional worship formats whether or not they help members experience God? The church that is known in its neighborhood for feeding and housing battered women, or the church that is unknown by its neighbors because it cannot find biblical authority for using church funds for such activities?"

Those who are part of this ground swell in the Churches of Christ are as passionate about restoration as those who have gone before. We are as taken with the power and vitality of the first-century church as were our parents. We, like them, believe that churches in Jerusalem and Antioch and Ephesus and—yes—even Corinth are worthy of our intense study and faithful imitation.

The difference is that we want most to restore the functions to which God has called his people, and are willing to disconnect first-century forms from those timeless functions. We believe it is possible to experience again the power and life-changing dynamic of the early church, but only if we are able to find fresh wineskins to contain the gospel that is always new.

We want the chance to build a church that flies. In many ways, the church that results will not look like the ancient church. It will use forms and methods and approaches that would never have occurred to Christians in Philippi or Rome. It will draw from a contemporary toolbox rather than an exclusively ancient one. It will meet modern needs using a mix of methods both ancient and modern.

What that church will have in common with the first churches is a commitment to being the people God wants us to be, doing the work God gives us to do, living the lives God calls us to live. Our methods may vary, but our goals are the same. Our means may differ, but our ends are identical. Our forms will be fresh, but the same functions hold for us as for them.

We long for the chance to build a church that flies with the ancient church. From the outset, we confess that the church we envision will not fly like its first-century counterpart in every respect. But in the end, we believe it is a functioning church that is important to God—whatever forms that church adopts.

That is a goal that has, I believe, the power to capture the children of the Restoration Movement. It is an ideal bold enough to break into our paralysis and startle us once more into activity. It promises to breathe new life into people who have lost their way and forgotten their purpose. By rediscovering the ancient purposes that have always shaped God's people in the past, and committing to the pursuit of those purposes in the present, we have hope of remembering what we are about and resuming our interrupted activity.

*This chapter is adapted from Tim Woodroof, *A Church That Flies: A New Call to Restoration in Churches of Christ* (Orange, CA: New Leaf Books, 2000).

Notes

1. Oliver Sacks, *The Man Who Mistook His Wife for a Hat* (New York: Touchstone Books, 1998).

2. See Richard Hughes and Leonard Allen, *Illusions of Innocence: Protestant Primitivism in America, 1630-1875* (Chicago, IL: University of Chicago, 1988), 170ff. "[Alexander Campbell] proclaimed in the *Christian Baptist* in 1825 that 'just in so far as the ancient order of things, or the religion of the New Testament, is restored, just so far has the Millennium commenced.'"

2

"The Last Will and Testament of the Churches of Christ"

Rob McRay

"We *will*, that this body die, be dissolved, and sink into union with the Body of Christ at large; for there is but one body, and one Spirit, even as we are called in one hope of our calling."[1] With these words, Barton W. Stone and his colleagues disbanded the Springfield Presbytery only a year after they had formed it. Offering their reasons for this drastic step, they wrote:

> Therefore, from a principle of love to Christians of every name, the precious cause of Jesus, and dying sinners who are kept from the Lord by the existence of sects and parties in the church, they have cheerfully consented to retire from the din and fury of conflicting parties—sink out of the view of fleshly minds, and die the death.[2]

This "Last Will and Testament of the Springfield Presbytery" is a remarkable document, not merely because it is one of the founding documents of the Churches of Christ, but because of its revolutionary appeal for nondenominational Christianity. They were offering a bold answer to the endless schisms and bitter conflicts that had fragmented the church since the Reformation.

The Churches of Christ were born out of a desire to present a radical alternative to the denominational divisions and dissension that had dominated Christianity for centuries. The vision of free congregations owing allegiance to no creed but Christ, beholding to no tradition save that handed down in the Scriptures, and wearing no names except those worn by Christians in the New Testament inspired generations of church leaders and members. The rhetoric of nondenominational Christianity profoundly shaped our self-perception. We are "New Testament Christians," "members of the Lord's church." We are not Methodists; we are "Christians." We do not belong to a church of Luther but to a "church of Christ." We have not joined a denomination; we have been "added by Christ to His church."

Our early leaders dreamed of our movement as a mighty, swelling flood sweeping across the frontier, and eventually the world, washing away the pollution of denominationalism and leaving in its wake countless congregations practicing pure, biblical Christianity. It was an exciting, zeal-inspiring dream. But the movement was still young when something began to go wrong with the dream. In 1840 Walter Scott wrote to a fellow preacher:

> When you express your doubts of the matters connected with the recent Reformation, I sympathize with you, for the thing has not been what I hoped it would be by a thousand miles. We are indeed "a sect" differing but little, of anything that is good, from the parties around us. Alas! My soul is grieved every day.[3]

Scott was reacting to the signs of sectarianism rising in the fellowship. Voices were no longer merely calling for all Christians to unite on the basis of the Bible alone; they were asserting that those who were thus following the Bible alone were alone Christians. A separate and distinct association of churches was forming that appeared little different than the denominations whom they castigated for being separate and distinct associations.

Still, the vision and rhetoric continued to find life and expression in our movement. By the end of the century, division had carved the

Churches of Christ into a separate fellowship from the rest of the movement. Our side of the fellowship still repeated the rhetoric of nondenominational Christianity, but the primary emphasis was on the absolute necessity of following the biblical pattern in order to truly be the Lord's church. Our most unique identity marker, a cappella singing, was both a product of, and a significant incentive for the preservation of, this emphasis on the biblical pattern. Issue after issue would continue to divide our churches and narrow the recognized boundaries of the true church.

On the other side of the instrumental music split, the sectarian impulse was not as strong. In 1899 J. H. Garrison published a paper on "The World's Need of Our Plea," in which he remained optimistic that our movement could resist the pressures to become a denomination.

> It remains to be seen whether this movement holds within itself the indestructible elements of freedom and progress. Three or four scores of years is too short a time, perhaps, for fully testing its capacity to resist all the temptations which usually beset a religious reformation, and tend to divert it from its original aim, but so far it has shown sufficient vitality and loyalty to its basic principle to overcome whatever tendency there has been to crystallize into a sect and make further progress heresy.[4]

I doubt Garrison could have written those words a century later. Our movement has not only evolved into a denomination, it has evolved into at least three denominations. The Disciples of Christ have openly accepted and affirmed this transition. The Christian Churches/Churches of Christ and the noninstrumental Churches of Christ have been more resistant. In fact, the Churches of Christ have been adamant in claiming themselves still to be nondenominational. This claim is unfortunately at odds with reality.

The Churches of Christ as a Denomination

According to any recognized definition, Churches of Christ would be classified as a denomination. For example:

The word denomination is derived from a Latin word (*denominare*) meaning "to name." A denomination is an association or fellowship of congregations within a religion that have the same beliefs or creed, engage in similar practices and cooperate with each other to develop and maintain shared enterprises.[5]

In the terms used by sociologists of religion, most mainstream Churches of Christ are clearly part of a denomination. "In the more precise typology of E. Troeltsch, denomination stands between the 'church type' and the 'sect type,' as a religious group accommodated to the prevailing culture, willingly accepting itself as one among many other denominations, stressing practical cooperation, and minimizing distinctive theological differences."[6]

According to this classification, our movement began as a sect and has been gradually evolving into a denomination.[7] In the late 1970s, Bill Humble told his Restoration History class at Abilene Christian University that we were most accurately defined as an "established sect," in between the "sect" and "denomination" categories but very close to becoming a denomination. We have now virtually completed that transition. Only the sectarian right wing of our fellowship might still make some claim to the more technical classification of "established sect"; but this distinction would be lost on most Christians.

At present, by virtually any definition of the term, we are clearly a denomination. Our institutions are denominational institutions; they exist to serve our fellowship within the confines of our tradition. They solicit funds from our churches to sponsor ministries to our churches or to our children, or to convert others to our churches, or to serve the poor in the name of our churches. The only way we can deny we are a denomination is to define the term in a way no one else defines it. We must sadly confess that we have become that which we once despised.

The simplest definition of a denomination is a group that is denominated, i.e., that distinguishes itself from other groups by a particular name. Churches of Christ clearly have done that—so much so, that when a congregation chooses to use some other name, they are suspected of heresy and accused of wanting to break with the Churches

"The Last Will & Testament of the Churches of Christ"

of Christ. Churches must consider what they mean when they put "Church of Christ" on the sign.

The term "Church of Christ" can be used in at least three ways. The first of these is the nondenominational sense, referring to the body of Christ at large. Thomas Campbell used it in this way in the first two of his propositions in the "Declaration and Address" of 1809:

> 1. That the church of Christ upon earth is essentially, intentionally, and constitutionally one; consisting of all those in every place that profess their faith in Christ and obedience to him in all things according to the scriptures....
>
> 2. That although the church of Christ upon earth must necessarily exist in particular and distinct societies, locally separate one from another; yet there ought to be no schisms, no uncharitable divisions among them.[8]

It can also be used in this way of local congregations as churches that belong to Christ, as in Romans 16:16. At the beginning of our movement, names like Church of Christ, Church of God, Christian Church and Disciples of Christ were all used as general terms for the greater church of our Lord, of which individual congregations saw themselves as merely a part.

The second use of the term "Church of Christ" is in a sectarian sense. In this sense, "Church of Christ" is used of a particular fellowship of churches with a particular heritage and particular shared identifying practices. Furthermore, the term is used interchangeably with expressions like "the Lord's church," indicating that this particular fellowship is the only true church, the sole continuation of the church of the New Testament. To be within the fellowship of the "Churches of Christ" is to be part of the body of Christ, and to be outside this fellowship is to be in a denomination of human making.

This approach denies that the Churches of Christ are part of a religious tradition that originated on the early nineteenth-century American frontier. Rather, as inscriptions on many church buildings declare, Churches of Christ are considered to be the original church founded by God on Pentecost in 33 A.D. In answering the charge that the Churches of Christ have become a denomination, sectarians would rebut that we are not a denomination because Jesus did not found a denomination. But this argument assumes its conclusion. The assertion is only true if one accepts the claim that the fellowship of the Churches of Christ and the church of the New Testament are in fact one and the same.

A third use of the term "Church of Christ" is as a denominational label. In this sense the term is used to designate congregations and institutions as belonging to a particular denomination among other denominations. Just as we speak of a Baptist Church or a Baptist college, we can speak of a Church of Christ or a Church of Christ college. The term is even used in phrases that might make a grammarian bristle, as in "Are you Church of Christ?" Using the term in this way acknowledges the historical reality that our fellowship has become a denomination much like any other.

Though sectarians among us still object, for the past several decades a rising chorus of voices has acknowledged this transformation of our movement. Despite our rhetoric, despite our desire to see ourselves as nondenominational, many among us know that our reality does not match our rhetoric. A growing number of our leaders and members would now argue that we not only are a denomination, but that we should embrace this reality and be responsible denominationalists. The transition from sect to denomination, they would argue, is inevitable. Rather than try to undo this evolution, we should strive to preserve what is good and unique about our heritage.

These new denominationalists (I use this phrase to distinguish them from the older sectarian position) would not argue that we are the only ones going to heaven. They would not contend that Churches of Christ are the only ones who can claim to be the Lord's church. They are willing to rethink issues of hermeneutics, theology and even tradition when necessary. Yet they would also resist a Church of Christ losing its distinctive identity and becoming another nondenominational evangelical community church. Tradition is valued as a means of preserving and passing on what we hold dear, and so they remain committed to many of the theological and ecclesiastical traditions of our heritage. They would reject the sectarianism that regards other denominations as heretical or hypocritical and would respect their perspectives and contributions. Our denomination, they would say, has as much right to exist and as much to contribute as any other.

These new denominationalists are *prima facie* evidence of our transition into a denomination. My quarrel is not with their assessment of our fellowship as a denomination, but with their acceptance and defense of this situation. That the Churches of Christ have become a denomination is irrefutable; but whether this move is inevitable, irreversible and desirable is certainly open to question.

The Demise of Denominationalism

American Christianity is undergoing a major transition. The great walls of tradition and peculiarity that divided denominations are crumbling. Families today choose churches based on other factors than loyalty to a denomination's creed, tradition and doctrine. We are entering what many call a post-denominational era in American churches. In *The Restructuring of American Religion*, Robert Wuthnow convincingly demonstrated that denominational distinctives are becoming less important and Christians are moving freely back and forth across once rigid denominational lines.[9]

Wuthnow observed that American Christians are realigning along a liberal-conservative axis. This can be seen in differing theological views as well as differing social and political views. It can also be demonstrated in the different kinds of parachurch organizations and small groups members join.[10] The difference between Methodists and Pres-byterians is becoming less important than the differences between liberals and conservatives within each denomination. Conservatives in various denominations are more likely to hold similar views and attend similar kinds of small groups than are liberals within the same denomination, and vice versa.

Several denominations whose leaders have tended toward the liberal end of the spectrum have seen the formation of more conservative grassroots movements within their memberships. For example, the

Disciples of Christ has Disciples Renewal and the Presbyterian Church (U.S.A.) has the Presbyterian Coalition. In fact, the Presbyterians also have the Covenant Network of Presbyterians on the other end of the spectrum from the Coalition, each organization created in the battle over the ordination of practicing homosexuals.

> The evolution of these two large, broadly based groups shows the evolution of "postdenominationalism" in the old mainline Protestant churches. Decline in denominational loyalty and the demise of denominational hegemony have been apparent for years. These realities, reinforced by the triumph of market consumerism throughout the culture, have led to the multiplication of special-interest groups throughout the church.[11]

At one end of the spectrum, mainline denominations of a more liberal perspective have been openly seeking unity through ecumenical efforts. This has led to varying degrees of union and cooperation. The Disciples of Christ and the United Church of Christ have been pursing merger, and the Evangelical Lutheran Church in America and the Episcopal Church have sought mutual recognition of each other's ordinations.

The Promise Keepers movement, which began in 1990, has primarily been composed of Christians from the more conservative end of the spectrum. This parachurch men's ministry has among its chief objectives the breaking down of denominational barriers. One of the most dramatic events in church history was the clergy conference in Atlanta in 1996, where approximately 40,000 pastors from virtually every denomination gathered to seek spiritual revival and Christian unity. The keynote lecture on unity was delivered by Max Lucado, a minister from the Churches of Christ.

In the mid-90s, while serving as minister of the Northtown Church in Milwaukee, I began attending the local ministerial association. The other participants were all from mainline Protestant denominations or Roman Catholics. On Palm Sunday evening we joined together in leading an ecumenical worship service. I was the only nondenominational minister, the only one from a believers' baptism tradition, and the only conservative evangelical. Following the clergy conference, I received an invitation to attend a new ministers' prayer group being formed by some who had also attended the event. This group was made up almost entirely of Pentecostals, Baptists and other Fundamentalists. I was the least conservative of these ministers. These two groups exemplify each side of Wuthnow's restructured American church. Denominational lines were being crossed at either end, but there was little unity between the two groups.

My youngest brother, Barrett McRay, has degrees in theology from the nondenominational Wheaton College. He has served as a youth minister in both a Lutheran church and a Presbyterian church, though he is neither a Lutheran nor a Presbyterian. Both congregations are on the evangelical side of the spectrum, which proves to be a more important determiner of fellowship than denominational identity.

In Houston a movement of prayer for the city, called "Mission Houston," is uniting small groups of pastors all across the metro area. In the suburb of Katy, one such group of pastors has begun referring to their developing interdenominational fellowship as "the Katy Church."

Such experiences illustrate the post-denominational character of American Christianity. More and more churches and church members are decrying the divisions in the body of Christ. They are seeking ways to reach across the barriers, cooperate in ministry, join in worship and work toward greater unity.

Another feature of the changing face of American Christianity is the rising number of nondenominational churches. The best known is the huge Willow Creek Community Church near Chicago, a completely nondenominational, evangelical congregation that has inspired a new approach to evangelism in our culture. In almost every city some of the largest and fastest growing churches are unaffiliated with any denomination. These nondenominational "community churches" can be found across the theological spectrum.

A related phenomenon is seen in denominational churches that downplay or even abandon their denominational identities and associations. For example, the Saddleback Valley Community Church near Los Angeles appears to most observers to be completely nondenominational, yet has the following statement in its bylaws: "This Church is autonomous and maintains the right to govern its own affairs, independent of any denominational control. Recognizing, however, the benefits of cooperation with other churches in world missions, this Church voluntarily affiliates with the Southern Baptist Convention in its national, state and local expressions." Increasingly common are church signs with a nondenominational name, such as "Community Church," and a denominational affiliation printed in smaller type. This trend is striking evidence of the waning attraction of denominations and the growing desire of Christians to simply be Christians.

Choosing the Future

At the very time when American Christianity is moving away from denominational affiliations toward nondenominational identities, it is sadly ironic that Churches of Christ are moving in the opposite direction. Just when churches up and down the street are re-evaluating their denominational status and seeking to be more nondenominational, many among us are abandoning the goal of nondenominational Christianity and seeking to be more like other denominational churches. Just as Christians all around us have become open to our movement's original vision, we are preparing to leave it behind. In our quest to end our sectarian isolation from the larger Christian church, we are giving up the part of our heritage that could provide the strongest ground for dialogue and interaction with other fellowships.

This is no time to accept the inevitability of our transition into a denomination. That we have become what we once despised is undeniable; but to accept and perpetuate this sad state of affairs would be tragic. To choose to be a denomination and preserve our heritage is in itself a denial of our heritage. Our movement was not called into being by the vision of a denomination demarcated by unaccompanied singing, baptism by immersion, weekly communion and a plurality of elders. Rather, the dream that gave birth to the Churches of Christ was of independent congregations of Christ's church practicing simple, Biblical, nodenominational Christianity. To choose to be a denomination is to choose to preserve our traditions while abandoning our core identity.

"The Last Will & Testament of the Churches of Christ"

The dream of nondenominational Christianity is now attracting more and more churches from a variety of traditions. This is no time to abandon the dream. This is a time for our churches and institutions to consider what it would really mean to recover our vision and claim with integrity to be nondenominational Christians. Our colleges must choose whether they want to be nondenominational like Wheaton College or Fuller Theological Seminary or denominational like Southern Methodist University or Southwestern Baptist Theological Seminary. The consequences of this choice will be dramatic, affecting recruiting, fund-raising and employment. It will affect lectureships and church relations and intern programs. But integrity demands that the choice be made. They must either abandon the vision and vocabulary of our nondenominational heritage or abandon their sectarian and denominational identities. Our benevolent ministries must choose whether they will be more like such nondenominational charities as World Vision or more like denominational agencies such as the Wisconsin Lutheran Child and Family Service. The choice will affect constituencies and partnerships and staffing, but the choice must be made.

Our congregations must make a choice whether they will be autonomous nondenominational congregations, as we have claimed to be, or denominational churches like so many of their neighboring churches—churches we once criticized for their denominational affiliations. The choice will affect what we teach our children and our converts about our identity. It will affect our fellowship with other churches, both from our own heritage and beyond. It will affect what we put on the sign, whether in large type or small, and what we mean by what we write there. Yet the choice must be made. Each church must choose to be true to our original vision and plea or loyal to the denominational boundaries and identity that have evolved. Neither is a choice to entirely abandon our heritage in Churches of Christ; but either option necessarily chooses one aspect of our heritage and rejects another. We cannot be nondenominational and denominational at the same time.

Unless we are prepared to defend the sectarian position that Churches of Christ are indeed the Lord's church, then we must acknowledge that we have become a denomination, "differing but little, of anything that is good, from the parties around us." And acknowledging that fact, we must choose to accept what we have become or to seek what we once longed to be. Now is the time to make the choice. If we choose denominationalism we may well be choosing a path of slow demise in this post-denominational era. If we choose nondenominationalism, the road will be uncertain and at times rocky, but the future will be hopeful and the dream inspiring. Now is the time for heirs of Stone's vision to take up pen and prayer and to write the "Last Will and Testament of the Churches of Christ":

> We *will*, that this body die, be dissolved, and sink into union with the Body of Christ at large; for there is but one body, and one Spirit, even as we are called in one hope of our calling.

Notes

1. Charles A. Young, *Historical Documents Advocating Christian Union* (1904; reprint ed., Joplin, MO: College Press, 1985), 20.

2. Ibid., 25.

3. Richard T. Hughes, *Reviving the Ancient Faith: The Story of Churches of Christ in America* (Grand Rapids, MI: Eerdmans, 1996), 54.

4. Young, 362.

5. David O. Moberg, "Denominationalism," in *Dictionary of Christianity in America*, ed. Daniel Reid, Robert Linder and Bruce Shelley (Downers Grove, IL: InterVarsity Press, 1990), 350.

6. N. H. Maring, "Denomination," in *Encyclopedic Dictionary of Religion*, ed. Paul Kevin Meagher, Thomas C. O'Brien and Consuelo Maria Ahern (Washington, D.C.: Corpus Publishing, 1979), 207.

7. For a helpful discussion of these terms as they apply to Churches of Christ, see Hughes' *Reviving the Ancient Faith*, 4-5.

8. Young, 107-8.

9. Robert Wuthnow, *The Restructuring of American Religion: Society and Faith Since World War II* (Princeton: Princeton University, 1988), 88ff.

10. Wuthnow, *Restructuring*, 219.

11. Joseph D. Small, "Signs of the Postdenominational Future," *Christian Century* (May 5, 1999), 509.

Church

3

Our Enduring Priesthood

Linda King

When I hear the word "priest," my first response is a visual image, a mental montage of tonsured monks, bearded rabbis, parish pastors in simple robes and mitred bishops in ornately embroidered vestments. In my pictorial glossary, I see a desert tabernacle, Solomon's temple, St. Peter's Basilica and St. Paul's Cathedral. I imagine the smell of incense and the sound of plainchant and the dark mahogany of ancient confessionals. What I don't see are the words "Church of Christ." And yet. And yet, the priesthood of all believers is a bedrock belief in Churches of Christ. Beyond the reach of debate, it seems as natural to us as breathing, so axiomatic that we scarcely notice it. More than an abstract concept, it undergirds and influences our church life in a thousand concrete ways.

Where did this doctrine come from? Why has this particular tenet been so important to us? What has made it such a good fit? How has it shaped who we are, what we do and how we do it? And how might it serve and instruct us in the future? These questions deserve our attention as the church looks back on two thousand years of history and steps across the threshold of a new century and millennium. For I believe that after the first principles of God's salvific love expressed through Christ, this concept of the priesthood of all believers is our strongest, most universally held, most powerful belief. More than all our other identifying marks, it is the best of what we as a Christian fellowship bring to the table, and it promises to endure and guide us in the uncharted waters ahead.

The Basis of the Belief

As with all the core teachings in the Churches of Christ, the first source of our belief lies in scripture, in the pages of the Old and New Testaments which we trust as the inspired word of God. As a people of the Book, we are known for our study of the Bible. So while they don't make our Top Ten list of memory verses or proof texts, the scriptures concerning a general priesthood probably sound familiar to us.

In Exodus 19:5-6 (*NIV*), the Lord spoke to His people through Moses, saying: "Now if you obey me fully and keep my covenant, then out of all nations you will be my treasured possession. Although the whole earth is mine, you will be for me a kingdom of priests and a holy nation . . . ." That this priesthood refers to the True Israel is clear from Isaiah's messianic prophecy about the year of the Lord's favor: "And you will be called priests of the Lord, you will be named ministers of our God" (Isa. 61:6, NIV). However, the most well known scriptural references to the priesthood of believers are from the New Testament. The Apostle Peter wrote to the scattered elect:

> As you come to him, the living Stone—rejected by men but chosen by God and precious to him—you also, like living stones, are being built into a spiritual house to be a holy priesthood, offering spiritual sacrifices acceptable to God through Jesus Christ . . . [Y]ou are a chosen people, a royal priesthood, a holy nation, a people belonging to God, that you may declare the praises of him who called you out of darkness into his wonderful light. (1 Pet. 2:4-5, 9, *NIV*)

The Revelation of John contains three fascinating allusions to Christian priesthood. In Revelation 1:5-6, John offers his opening doxology "to him who loves us and has freed us from our sins by his blood, and has made us to be a kingdom and priests to serve his God and Father." Later, when the four living creatures and the 24 elders fall down before the Lamb, they sing a new song:

> You are worthy to take the scroll and to open its seals,
>   because you were slain,
> and with your blood you purchased men for God
> from every tribe and language and people and nation.
> You have made them to be a kingdom and priests to
>   serve our God,
> and they will reign on the earth. (Rev. 5:9-10, *NIV*)

And for those who have part in the first resurrection, "The second death has no power over them, but they will be priests of God and of Christ and will reign with him for a thousand years" (Rev. 20:6, *NIV*).

In between the early promise of a royal priesthood in Exodus and John's late vision of Christians as kings and priests in Revelation are a number of scriptures which depict Christians as performing the role and function of priests: approaching the presence of God, offering sacrifices, declaring the praise of God to the people, serving in the Holy Place. Some of these priestly references use symbols and metaphors; others are part of a typological comparison of the Old Covenant and the New Covenant. Taken together, they comprise a doctrine that exists in some form across the centuries[1] and throughout Christendom: that because Jesus Christ is King of Kings as well as the great High Priest, all Christians partake somehow in the kingly and priestly nature of Christ, with both the privileges and the responsibilities attendant thereto.

The Appeal of the Belief

The idea of a universal priesthood may be as old as the book of Exodus, but it was a perfect fit for the Restoration Movement. With a hermeneutic based on common-sense rationalism and the rugged individualism which characterized the American frontier spirit, our forebears found the simplicity and democracy of each-person-a-priest to be naturally appealing, fair and in harmony with how they saw the world. The orderly type-and-antitype comparison of priestly service under the Old and New Covenants, set out in detail in the letter to the Hebrews, seemed logical and symmetrical. Everyone knew that repression by clergy and restraint of freedom of worship had been among the ills that motivated the settling of the New World. Surely, reasoned early American believers, the freedom of religious belief and the preservation of individual rights upon which this nation was founded derived from no less than the Holy Scriptures themselves. Eschewing titles and clerical hierarchies, therefore, our early preachers stressed the personal accountability of each believer: to study like the Bereans, to rightly handle the word of God, to live a righteous life and to evangelize. Not only did each individual stand alone before God, each congregation stood alone. These historic corollaries of the priesthood of all believers have shaped our self-concepts as individuals and our practice as churches in ways that are biblical and wholesome, life-giving and wise. But they have also fallen victim to distortion and abuse in ways that foster pride, ignorance, rebellion and chaos.

The Power and Influence of the Belief

Our Relationship with God

If all Christians are priests, then each Christian is a priest.[2] If each Christian is a priest, then we each have direct access to God through the one Mediator, Christ Jesus, described in Hebrews 8:1 as our High Priest under the new covenant. This is the chief privilege of priesthood. Just as we must all give account of ourselves before God (Rom. 14:12), we may, and indeed must, draw near to God personally, offering our prayers and spiritual sacrifices to Him through Christ. We cannot have a vicarious relationship with the Lord; we cannot delegate or designate or defer to another human to do it for us. In this sense, ours is a do-it-yourself faith. However, the exposition in Hebrews 8-10 leaves no doubt that our redemption, our installation into priesthood, our service in the Holy Place as priests, and our ultimate joining of Christ in the Most Holy Place in the presence of God are all made possible solely by the blood of Christ, who gave himself for us. Thus, the first glorious significance of the priesthood of all believers is that each individual is called by the gospel to enter into a personal relationship with God. As members of Churches of Christ, we believe this viscerally; we cherish this privilege as our birthright as sons and daughters of God. We fall on our knees in confession and prayer to God, rather than man; we most often seek divine wisdom and guidance by inquiring directly of God, rather than seeking the collective wisdom of the church or any of its members. Notwithstanding certain scriptural passages about keys to the kingdom and the power to bind and loose, we shudder to think of seeking absolution from any human or institution or granting the forgiveness of sins to another.

The dangers that accompany this direct access to Almighty God are many. Because "[I]t is a dreadful thing to fall into the hands of the living God" (Heb. 10:31 NIV), priests must be careful to approach our Creator with sincere hearts and full assurance of faith, remembering that it is by the blood of Christ that we are sanctified to serve. There is no room for pride. As in all relationships, confidence and intimacy can foster the natural tendencies to grow casual, careless, presumptuous or trite. But the writer of Hebrews warns the priesthood of believers to "[B]e thankful, and so worship God acceptably with reverence and awe, for our 'God is a consuming fire'" (Heb. 12:29, *NIV*). Without the imposition of such external barriers as a rood screen, a liturgy performed in a foreign language, or a Eucharistic cup not shared with the worshippers, it becomes the privilege of each priest to be bold but humble. Without the addition of such awe-inspiring sights and sounds as a magnificent cathedral, a high altar, beautiful stained glass windows, sculpture, tapestries, and mysterious echoing chants, it becomes the duty of each priest to remain awe-full.

A more subtle misapplication of the universal priesthood is that the individual believer can thereby feel insecure, alone, at sea. Cyril Eastwood's description of the Puritans sometimes fits us rather well.[3] Like the Puritans before us, we can focus on the idea that "alone we face God and alone we face hell. We suffer the terrors of the medieval Christian without the comforts."[4] Without the massive power of the

Roman Church, without the quiet contentment of the true Calvinist who believes that he was predestined to be saved, we struggle for the assurance of the Lutheran that faith alone is quite sufficient, and we feel compelled to buttress faith with our will, our reasoning and our effort. We are desperate to "get it right."

Our Relationship with the Scriptures
Another important aspect of the priesthood of all believers is its effect on how we treat the scriptures. In the ancient church, the Bible was not available to the laity. Bibles were written in Latin and the common person could not read the word of God for himself. For many centuries, therefore, the message of the scriptures was mediated through the church and its clergy. After the English Bible appeared in the 1500s, thanks to such heroes of the Reformation as Thomas Cranmer, God's word could speak directly to prelate and peasant alike. It has been said that "[N]o single incident in our history has done more to implement the Reformation doctrine of the Priesthood of all Believers than the introduction of the English Bible."[5]

We take this gift for granted, but it was a revolutionary event.

> It was wonderful to see with what joy this Book of God was received, not only among the learned sort, and those that were noted for lovers of the Reformation, but generally all England over, among all the vulgar and common people; and with what greediness God's Word was read; and what resort to places where the reading of it was. Everybody that could bought the book, and busily read it, and got others to read it to them; and divers more elderly people learned to read on purpose.[6]

And so it remains today in our churches. Perhaps without as much joy, surprise or enthusiasm, but with an enormous sense of respect and duty, we teach and practice the privilege of personal Bible study. For most of the twentieth century, members of Churches of Christ were described as Bible-toting and scripture-quoting. Whether this was praise or pejorative depended upon the circumstance. However, the point remains: we have always taken seriously, and personally, Paul's mandate to Timothy to "Study to shew thyself approved unto God, a workman that needeth not to be ashamed, rightly dividing the word of truth" (2 Tim. 2:15, *KJV*). We emphasize Bible reading at home; we recruit, train and honor excellent Bible teachers in our churches. Sometimes our motives have been mixed or less than noble. For a few decades mid-century, we studied and memorized diligently because we were afraid the Communists might wrest the Bibles from our hands or the new Roman Catholic president might discourage Bible study for all but the clergy. In my own Christian adolescence, I wish I had spent more time allowing the scriptures to instruct me and less time searching for how they could correct my neighbor. Nevertheless, as a group of believers, we in Churches of Christ no longer, if we ever did, use the Bible as an offensive weapon or a talisman to bless our particular agenda. Rather, we love the Bible, we respect and cherish it as the inspired word of God, we commit it to memory and write it on our hearts, and when we need it, we call up-on it for sustenance, solace, guidance and correction.

Again, however, there is a peril which accompanies the privilege. In our flight from the heresies of the past, in our fear of teaching as doctrine the commands of men, in our desire to allow each believer/priest to read for herself and respond to the scriptures according to conscience, we have sometimes gone too far. We have chosen to remain ignorant of the history and writings of the church, as if nothing of value to us occurred between A.D. 95 and the Stone-Campbell movement or as if the only two choices were worshipping the church traditions of the past or scorning them. Our church libraries, if we have them, are too often barren of anything written before 1850 or any treatise or commentary by authors outside the Restoration heritage. Our Christian colleges and universities, until recent years, have required little in the way of church history or hermeneutics. Therefore, our believer/priests, even the educated ones, tend to approach the scriptures with a naiveté and unexamined, optimistic crudity that borders on arrogance. "Ah, it's easy," we seem to be saying. "Anyone can do this without much effort." It is almost as if we place the scriptures under glass, hermetically sealed and protected from centuries of diligent study, and then throw open the doors to our priceless treasure and invite the clumsy, the casual and the curious to wander in and have a go. No wonder that simplistic, shallow and emotionally exploitative religious guidebooks sell well on the bookshelves today. We have underestimated the capacity of our believer/priests by not developing in them a taste for the weightier ideas, a hunger for understanding beyond first principles, and an appreciation of the connection between ourselves and all believers in all times and all places.

Our Relationship with the Church
An old nursery rhyme goes, "Here's the church. Here's the steeple. Open the door, and see all the people." Well, not so in the Churches of Christ. Perhaps more than all our Christian neighbors, we recognize and frequently remark that the church is not a building: it's the people—the Lord's people, the body of Christ—whether inside or outside the building. Every child in our midst knows that we don't vote members into the church and people don't join the church like they join a civic club. Rather, we teach and practice the message of Acts 2:47; that is, the Lord adds to the church daily those who are being saved. And once inside the church, there is no hierarchy. We are all priests.

That belief is reflected in our buildings. Yes, they're plain, and sometimes even homely. Utilitarian rather than lofty, beautiful or awe-inspiring. We have no chancel, no quire, no altars. There is no bishop's chair, no seat of authority, no place of exclusivity off-limits to the laity. At least within our congregations, we truly believe in a diversity of gifts and ministries but one body, with all parts essential.

The universal priesthood also influences our church organization and governance. Following instructions in the letters to Timothy and Titus, we appoint our leaders from among ourselves. Our elders/bishops/pastors and deacons are ordinary laymen rather than seminary-trained and ordained clergy. In fact, the ordination of clergy is practically non-existent among our congregations. Because we believe that all Christians are ministers of reconciliation and Christ's ambassadors, we make little or no distinction between clergy and laity insofar as authority and duty are concerned. Nor do we have a uniform liturgy. Each congregation, under the leadership of its elders and deacons and the service of its ministers, decides for itself what to study, how and where to serve, and what to practice in its gathered assemblies.

The best outgrowth of this non-hierarchical view of how we "do church" is a broad volunteer spirit. Bible classes, benevolence works, even evangelistic efforts are understood to be the responsibility of every believer/priest. "If it is to be, it's up to me," we often say to ourselves. This attitude promotes an active faith. It makes us doers of the word, and not hearers only. It gives us an appreciation of the contributions made by our fellow Christians and a sense of responsibility to discover and use our own individual talents for the Lord's service. Rather than being part of a Sunday morning audience, we are part of a Sunday morning communal service. This attitude partly explains our reluctance to use choirs or dramatic performances in our worship assemblies. For centuries in the ancient church, the worship or mass was a ritual performed only by priests and clergy. The parishioners were mere observers, while the priests recited the texts and sang the chants in Latin, said the prayers and reserved the communion cup for themselves.

We practice the polar opposite. In fact, our weekly open communion is one of the most beautiful features of our church assemblies. Across the country and around the world, we invite whosoever will to come and celebrate with us at the Lord's Table. We acknowledge that we are all unworthy and can attend the feast only because we are dressed in the clothes of our brother, Jesus. We have put on Christ. Over the years, there have been too many occasions when we in Churches of Christ have appeared to our neighbors to be sanctimonious, sectarian and exclusive. Somehow, though, by the grace of God, we have never given up our practice of open communion. May it ever be thus.

Nevertheless, the practice of a general priesthood can produce unintended consequences in our churches. If the priesthood is seen as more of a privilege than a responsibility, an individual may get an inflated view of himself and his own ideas. Like Miriam in the Old Testament or the sons of Zebedee in the New Testament, we are tempted to assert ourselves, to insist on parity, if not prominence, among our peers. It is easy to be like the priests Hophni and Phinehas, to stick our forks in and grab the best for ourselves. It is difficult to be like our High Priest Jesus and become a servant of many. We have a long way to go in learning to submit to one another out of reverence for Christ.

Moreover, the universal priesthood may suggest to some that all ideas, opinions, interpretations and understandings are equally valid. Our populist frontier heritage has a bit of anti-intellectualism built into it anyway, so we tend to disregard or undervalue the worth of a seminary education or other formal study of theology or ministry. We become supicious of too much learning, thereby depriving ourselves of the benefit of countless hours of study and years of experience by the scholars and veterans among us.

Dispute resolution can also become a problem. When there is a loose, informal and unwieldy structure of committees, business meetings, ministers, deacons and elders, and little formal communication of procedures, trying to solve a simple problem can be frustrating. Efficiency is rare; confusion and miscommunication are common. The result can be unpredictability, discouragement, mistrust, anger or apathy. Given the mobility of modern American society and the variations among congregations, incoming church members may learn to their dismay that methods and procedures accepted at their previous congregation are not even tolerated at the new congregation, and vice versa. Such upheavals take an emotional and spiritual toll on the congregants.

In addition, the belief in an autonomous local church made up of individual believer/priests can have the ironic effect of fostering transience and disloyalty. Since we have no official parishes, either by geography or assignment, each person is free to select a congregation of choice. Particularly in urban areas, where many choices exist, church shopping and swapping become commonplace. That is, individual Christians may reason that since they carry their priesthood wherever they go, they are free to go anywhere and everywhere they like. There is little sense of congregational loyalty, continuity or unity. If the preacher says something that offends, they go elsewhere. If the elders embark on a path or program they don't like, they move to the church across town. Sometimes, this attitude reflects a proud and rebellious heart, but more often it is innocent. Nevertheless, this practice of transience, even among faithful Christians, undermines the leadership of the congregation, increases anxiety and weakens the relational ties that make up body life in the church. *Koinonia* can scarcely exist among strangers, so worshippers tend to leave feeling lonely and disconnected, or they supplant genuine fellowship with manufactured intimacy.7 The "alone together" phenomenon is well documented in modern church and sociological studies. How to re-place it with true fellowship remains a challenge.

The Priesthood in My Congregation

The foregoing observations about the priesthood of believers are all apparent in the small congregation of which I am a part. For 18 years we have been an all-volunteer church, with no paid staff except a part-time youth minister and part-time custodian. We don't oppose paid ministers; surely the laborer is worthy of his hire. We have simply made the choice that we will do all we can ourselves. The good news is that there is an enormous sense of inclusion, of participation, of personal accountability to God and to one another. Our youth know that they are valued, respected, listened to and cared about. We have all-church meetings which address everything from meeting times to doctrinal disagreements. We have open committees and ministries, and every member is encouraged to participate. We have learned that ideas are better implemented when they spring up at a grassroots level than when they are imposed by church elders. We have a genuine appreciation for the unique gifts and perspective of each individual part of the body.

Nowhere is this more apparent than in our Sunday morning assemblies. We have no pews or podium; our chairs are usually placed in concentric circles so we can see and edify one another. Once a quarter we pass around a sign-up sheet for volunteers to plan our Sunday morning communion hours. Every believer/priest (man, woman, teenager, boy, girl, Sunday School class, family) is welcome to sign up. Then, with appropriate help from our worship committee, the volunteer plans it all: chooses a theme, selects the scriptures, chooses the songs, and then recruits the people who will lead prayers and songs, make comments, serve communion and collect the offering. This practice requires us all to be flexible and to appreciate variety. For example, one week the service may be rather "high church," with King James scriptures, staid hymns and a serene pace and order. Another week, it may seem more like a tent meeting on the wrong side of the tracks, with songs straight off country-western radio and sentiments that evoke 1950s Texas. The next week our teens might plan a service that feels like summer camp, with contemporary Christian songs, upbeat tempos and informal testimonies. Of course, each of us prefers one style more than others, but we trust that God delights in them all. And we have grown to value, even cherish, the infinite variety of God's children and the amazing ways in which we can learn from one another. It is altogether shocking and wonderful to leave a service thinking, "Whew, I'm glad that's over. That kind of service does nothing for me," and to hear two other people saying how uplifting and inspiring it was. Besides, when each member plans a communion service himself or herself, we can at least appreciate how much work goes into the preparation, so we are far less likely to complain.

Our congregation's missionaries have always come from among our own ranks, and we encourage all our members to take part in summer mission projects and community service. When we last appointed elders, we had a ceremony in which the elders took basin and towel and washed the feet of representative members of the congregation. The symbolic message was clear: we are your servant leaders; we will not be lords over you.

This radical, perhaps outrageous, experiment in living out the priesthood of all believers has had its costs. Sometimes the disorganization has veered too close to chaos. Sometimes the responsibility of speaking the truth to one another in love has been a heavy weight. Sometimes the best of our workers grow weary in well-doing. Often we make mistakes, fail, hurt one another and are called upon to forgive. But even in those times, we bless the name of the Lord. As good priests should.

The Future of the Belief

No one can say what the new millennium will hold for the Church of Christ as we know it. Surely some of its practices and emphases will change. But this bedrock belief in the priesthood of all believers, based on the sacrifice of Christ our High Priest, should continue to guide our churches far into the future. If we teach our grandchildren that all believers are priests in the service of God, they will know that their relationship with God must be personal. They will share our sense of accountability but will find new ways to declare the mighty works of God with authority, confidence and humility. Perhaps their sense of universal priesthood will lead them to be more inclusive of the people in the bushes and on the sidelines: the women and children, the non-married, the poor and oppressed. Perhaps, better than we, they will reach out to all believers in the community and around the world, with cooperative ministries and pulpit exchanges and other opportunities to both teach and learn a more excellent way. And by offering up continual sacrifices of praise, prayer, thanksgiving and loving acts of kindness, this multitude of priests will declare the love of God to the world.

Still, a word of warning may be appropriate. Now that Churches of Christ have crossed the tracks into mostly suburban respectability and occasional affluence, there is a danger that we may drift away from the precious privilege of believer priesthood. Many of us no longer mow our own lawns, iron our own clothes, change the oil in our cars, or do our own heavy cleaning. We hire it done by others who do it well. After all, those tasks are hard and they take too much time. So it is with the priesthood, we may reason. It can be hard, it takes time and, besides, it carries too much responsibility. In this modern era of "professionalism and excellence," wouldn't it be better just to delegate these priestly roles to the experts? Wouldn't it be safer? But the answer, of course, is no. The only way to enter the Most Holy Place is for each of us who has been washed in the atoning blood of Christ to draw near as priests and offer our personal spiritual sacrifices in service to the living God.

Notes

1. The early apostolic fathers (including the Didache, Clement of Rome, Ignatius, and Polycarp) recognized the sacerdotal aspect of the Christian life and the need for all Christians to offer "spiritual sacrifices" to God, such as in worship, witness and service. With the third-century writings of Cyprian, however, the concept of a clerical priesthood attained dominance. See James Leo Garrett, "The Priesthood of all Christians," *Southwestern Journal of Theology* 30 (Spring 1988), 3-54. Thereafter, the doctrine received occasional mention but did not regain meaningful recognition until it was rediscovered and emphasized by Martin Luther in the mid-1500s. Since then, it has been a doctrinal mainstay of most Protestant denominations, figuring prominently in the theology of John Calvin, John Wesley and their progeny.

2. It has occasionally been opined that the priesthood of all believers refers only to the church as a collective body and not to individual believers. See the discussion by Ernest Best, "Spiritual Sacrifice: General Priesthood in the New Testament," *Interpretation* 14 (July 1960), 273-299, 295. However, most biblical scholars who have addressed this point conclude that it is the individual Christian who approaches God through Christ and who offers spiritual sacrifices.

3. See the discussion of the Puritan tradition in Cyril Eastwood, *The Priesthood of All Believers: An Examination of the Doctrine from the Reformation to the Present Day* (London: Epworth, 1960), 130-182.

4. Ibid., 151.

5. Ibid., 98.

6. C. G. McCrie, *Contemporary Portraits of Reformers*, as quoted in Eastwood, ibid., 98.

7. For example, forced self-disclosure, hyper-emotionalism and intrusion into a member's private life.

4

The Challenge of Worship Renewal

Randy Gill

That wallpaper has got to go."

The words were surprisingly painful. Although they knew it was necessary, John and Katherine didn't want to sell the house. The place was filled with memories. Every room showed their personal stamp. They had picked the carpet and the window treatments...and the wallpaper. There was a mark on the kitchen door for every year of their son's life. Now two strangers, a young couple who had never owned a home before, were standing in their living room talking about how they were going to change the house they loved.

"What's wrong with the place?" they wondered. "It looks fine to us just the way it is."

Sound familiar? It should.

Something similar is happening right now in many of our congregations. People who have spent their entire lives building and nurturing the church are anxiously watching a younger generation attempt to change things. It might be the new video screen in the auditorium or the increasingly casual dress of the preacher or song leader. It could be the small group of singers with microphones on the front row. Whatever form it might take, the result is fundamentally the same.

Worship doesn't look or feel like it used to. Somebody is changing the wallpaper and not everyone is happy about it.

Dramatic Changes

In the book of Ezra there's an interesting story about some older men struggling with something new. The Jews had been slaves in Babylon for years when the king decided to allow some of them to return to Jerusalem to rebuild the temple. When the foundation was laid, the people gathered to celebrate and offer praise to the Lord. "But many of the priests and Levites and family heads, who had seen the former temple, wept aloud when they saw the foundation of this temple being laid, while many others shouted for joy." According to Ezra, it was impossible to tell the difference between the weeping and the rejoicing because the people made so much noise (Ezra 3:12). Today, in many of our churches, a similar roar is being heard as those calling for worship reform compete with those crying out for the preservation of heritage and tradition.

In the past, in most of our congregations, we could expect things to be pretty much the same on any given Sunday. Our worship was predictable, a testimony to the "divine pattern" many of us believed scripture provided. Paul's instruction to the Corinthians to do things decently and in order was seen as a timeless directive regarding worship. Our Sunday morning services incorporated the same "five acts" every week—singing, praying, teaching, giving and communion. In most of our churches these activities followed a reliable and predetermined order. Since the New Testament has so little to say about the mechanics of corporate worship we have felt free on occasion to provide more specific guidelines to bring structure and order to our services. We have decided how many songs should be sung and in what order, whether communion should come before or after the sermon, even the proper time for announcements and the acceptable phraseology for public prayers. Over time these pragmatic choices have become a kind of unofficial liturgy.

The atmosphere of the service was also predictable. Restraint was a highly valued characteristic of the assembly. Singing could be spirited, particularly at special events, but emotion, in general, was discouraged. We didn't think much about enjoying worship. God had commanded us to praise him and our services were for his benefit, not ours. To suggest that our assemblies were boring or outdated would have been considered selfish.

Over the past several years the shape and substance of our corporate worship has changed considerably. For an increasing number of churches there is no such thing as a typical Sunday anymore. The order of the service is different from week to week. Great old hymns we have sung for generations are being used less or not at all, while contemporary "praise choruses" have taken center stage. Our song leaders have become "worship leaders." A "praise team" of additional singers is often used to provide musical support for the congregation and to teach new songs. Women are being given a more significant and visible role in our assemblies. We have become dependent on computers and video screens for song lyrics and Bible readings. Sermons are shorter and less formal. Drama sketches and movie clips are being used to enhance the teaching. In some of our congregations, choirs, solos and "presentation music" have become common. Everything about worship, from the music choices to the casual dress of the participants, seems dramatically different than it was a decade ago.

How did this happen?

Not surprisingly, the change began in the 1960s. One of the most significant legacies of that turbulent decade was a youth-driven revival known as the Jesus Movement. On college campuses, street corners and coffeehouses young Christians used music as a way of communicating the gospel to their peers and as a medium of expressive worship. Like the great revivals that had come before, they combined the message of Jesus with the popular music of the time. Unlike the spirited gospel songs of the 1920s, however, or the stately hymns of the 1800s this music sounded more like Bob Dylan or the Beatles. Among the Jesus People and in churches like Calvary Chapel in Costa Mesa, California, a new kind of worship song was born. Companies like Maranatha! and Integrity began to nurture songwriters and to produce recordings and sheet music that introduced their music to the larger, evangelical church. Across America a fresh style of praise and worship emerged as young people expressed themselves in music.[1]

Our teenagers heard these songs at camp or learned them at youth rallies and brought them back to their home congregations. They were musically simple, often unison or with an accompanying counter melody. Many of the lyrics came straight from scripture. Although some of our older members dismissed them as trite or repetitive, songs like Karen Lafferty's "Seek Ye First" eventually made their way into our repertoire. For many, they touched a nerve. Unlike much of the music we sang, these songs felt fresh and contemporary. They connected with people. This was a musical language many of us understood.

At the same time we were seeing a whole new approach to religion on television. The shows of TV evangelists like Oral Roberts, Jim Bakker and Jimmy Swaggart were attracting huge audiences and incredible financial support. Since most of these preachers were Pentecostal, their programs brought a new kind of worship into the living rooms of America. As LaMar Boschman observes, the Pentecostals seemed especially well suited for television. "Their worship had the right visual qualities: the action, dynamic singing and sense of drama that were new and intriguing to Christian America."[2] For many the TV images of people kneeling, raising hands or weeping as they worshiped opened a whole new world of possibilities.

By the 1970s the cultural move towards postmodernism was being felt in Catholic and Protestant churches alike. Robert Webber put it this way, "There is a great shift taking place in our Western world today—a shift away from the Newtonian world of mechanism and rationalism to a new concept of the world that recognizes movement and mystery at the very core of life....As a result, people are now considerably more open to the supernatural and are searching for an experience of mystery."[3] The emphasis on objectivity and reason that had characterized the previous generation was giving way to emotion and experience. Believers of all backgrounds found themselves feeling empty and dissatisfied. Ironically, that seemed to be especially true in their worship services. Rather than being passive spectators, watching a traditional liturgy unfold, they hungered for a sense of God's presence in their midst. A well-ordered, cerebral service was not what they needed. This desire for change eventually sparked a kind of "worship reformation" that has swept the world over the past twenty years. With it has come an outpouring of new music, a greater freedom in the physical expression of worship, a desire for inclusion and participation in the assembly, and a spirit of abandon and celebration that is new to many traditions.

Changes among Churches of Christ

In the past all of this would have had little effect on us. The belief that we were the only true church kept most of our members insulated from the beliefs and practices of the Baptists or the Presbyterians. Over the past decade, however, a growing number of people from Churches of Christ have begun venturing out into the religious world beyond their own walls. We have attended community services at Easter or Christmas. We have been part of inter-denominational Bible studies. We have attended workshops at "seeker friendly" churches like Willow Creek and Saddleback. Our men have gone to Promise Keepers and our women have participated in similar conferences. The Contemporary Christian Music industry has brought us together at concerts and festivals. The rapid growth of Christian publishing has made it possible for us to enjoy a rich and diverse smorgasbord of ideas through books and authors that cross denominational lines.

As a result of all of this a growing number of our churches have begun incorporating some of the things they have learned or experienced elsewhere into their own assemblies. They have made their services more casual and their music more contemporary in an effort to reach out to their culture. They have created an a cappella version of the worship team to help their members learn and sing new songs. They have developed drama ministries to provide teaching moments in their services that communicate quickly and effectively with non-church visitors. They have involved more of their members, including women, in public roles in order to encourage greater participation and to demonstrate that they honor the gifts of all their people. They use computers and video screens in order to communicate better with a technologically sophisticated audience.

The reaction to these changes has been mixed. Some congregations have chosen to ignore the "worship reformation" altogether. For them, these innovations are little more than passing fads—like religious hula hoops that are here today and gone tomorrow. Others have experimented with a new element here or there but have remained basically committed to a traditional format. Often changes are abandoned quickly at the first sign of criticism. A larger group has publicly attacked both contemporary worship and its advocates. Paying little attention to the concept of congregational autonomy, they have spoken out against change, not only in their own churches, but within the brotherhood as a whole. In pulpits, lecture programs and periodicals the criticism has been fierce, pointed and surprisingly personal. Many suggest that a painful split is inevitable unless those embracing and promoting contemporary worship return to the fold.

The simple truth is that some of our churches will never change their worship format. What they do on Sundays is the result of years of sincere Bible study and consistent with a long and proud heritage. It's meaningful to them and they see no need to change. It's equally true that those congregations who are moving towards a more contemporary style of worship are unlikely to go back to the way things used to be. They love the sense of freedom and celebration that characterizes their time together. They don't worry that their services may be confusing or seem old-fashioned to their friends and neighbors. They have tasted new wine and the old wineskins will never be adequate again.

However we may feel about it, the call for revival in worship is not going to go away. If there's going to be any hope for unity and peace among our churches in the years ahead, we are going to have to find a way to change the tone of our discussions about worship. In the past, people on both sides of the issue have had a tendency to be judgmental, arrogant and dismissive. Those advocating change have painted those who prefer a more traditional approach as hopelessly out-of-date and disinterested in reaching a lost world. They have characterized some of our older members as narrow minded and unwilling to move beyond their "comfort zones." The traditionalists, they have charged, are only interested in the preservation of obsolete worship practices, no matter how ineffective they are or how much they are alienating their own children. On the other hand, opponents of change have suggested that the reformers are more interested in satisfying their own "preferences" than they are in pleasing God. Rather than making their assemblies more accessible to "seekers," progressive churches have been "dumbing down" worship or transforming it into shallow entertainment. What they are doing, critics have suggested, is unbiblical and is leading the church towards even greater error around the corner.

There is no question that disagreement over worship has resulted in tension and discord in many of our congregations over the past decade. Unfortunately, the same thing is true in many of our families. It is not uncommon to hear parents and their adult children acknowledge that, in order to preserve peace at family gatherings, the subject of worship has to be intentionally avoided. It is a sad commentary that many of us can't talk to each other about praising God without ending up in a quarrel.

What do our "worship wars" say to the rest of the world? Jesus said that people will know we are his disciples by the way we love each other. For those outside our churches, who are trying desperately to find meaning and hope for their lives or comfort in the midst of suffering, our arguments over the value of songbooks or the appropriateness of a woman holding a microphone must be very confusing. It's hard for them to see the spirit of Christ in a church where people would threaten to leave if someone sings a solo or if communion comes before the sermon instead of after? What kind of message are we sending our own children when we openly ridicule the beliefs of their grandparents or the worship style of a more conservative church across town?

We are going to have to learn a new language if we are going to be able to talk to each other in a meaningful way about worship. Even in matters on which we disagree we need to fight the temptation to judge each other's hearts and motives. An attitude of humility, kindness and respect for one another would be so much more helpful than the sarcasm and condescension that has characterized the discussion so far.

Beyond Externals

In addition to changing our tone, we need to take a closer look at the real issues involved in worship renewal. In John 4 a Samaritan woman asks Jesus a question about worship. "Our fathers worshiped on Mount Gerazim," she says. "Your people worship in Jerusalem. Which of us is right?" In his answer Jesus tells her that her question is about to become irrelevant. "God is spirit," he says, and has never really been confined to a particular place. Through Jesus that transcendence is about to be demonstrated. From this point on God will dwell in the hearts of all who believe. The symbolism of the ceremonies and sacrifices of the past is about to be replaced by reality—the sacrifice of God's own son. What God is looking for now, Jesus says, is people who worship from the depths of their souls and who are willing to offer their lives daily as living sacrifices. It is not the externals that are important, he says, but the spirit.

It is a message the Old Testament prophets had been trying to communicate for generations. Isaiah condemned Israel for honoring God with their lips while their hearts were far from him (Isa. 29:13). Jeremiah reminded the people that when God delivered their ancestors from Egypt he was more interested in obedience than in burnt offerings and sacrifices (Jer. 7:22). Through Amos, God told Israel that he hated the hypocrisy of their worship and that he wouldn't listen to their songs of praise until he saw justice and righteousness in their lives (Amos 5:21-24). Jesus himself acknowledged that the Pharisees had the outward rituals and ceremonies of their religion down to an art but he called them "blind guides" and hypocrites.

So much of our conversation about worship shows a similar preoccupation with externals. Focusing on things like praise teams and projected song lyrics misses the bigger picture. We have to take the discussion to a deeper level. The issues raised by the worship renewal movement are more profound and more complicated than the style of music we use in our assemblies or whether a praise team is acceptable if it's seated on the front pew. We need to be asking more significant questions. What are we really hoping to accomplish when we come together? Is God really at the center of what we do? To what extent

The Challenge of Worship Renewal

have we turned human tradition into divine ordinance? How can we hope to have truly meaningful corporate worship when so few of our people are experiencing personal worship during the week? How much studying and teaching are we doing about worship in our churches and in our homes? What are our colleges and universities doing to prepare future preachers and worship leaders for the roles they will have in our congregations when they graduate?

Many churches leaders have become so entrenched in their desire to preserve tradition that they fail to recognize the motivation behind the calls for reform. Too often the issues upon which they stand are not really the issues at all. We need to be asking why so many people feel the need for change rather than concentrating on the changes themselves. In a recent study George Barna asked people who attended church on a regular basis how often they experienced the presence of God in their worship services. Sixty-one per cent answered "rarely" or "never."[4] We need to be asking if that's true in our churches and, if it is, what we ought to be doing about it.

On the other hand, those who have plunged "heart first" into worship renewal need to be asking some tough questions as well. Has genuine worship been replaced in our assemblies by entertainment? Have we become too enamored with and dependent on technology? Are we placing an unhealthy emphasis on emotional response? Have we overemphasized joy and celebration while ignoring the importance of reverence and reflection? Are we watering down the message of Christ in our sermons and songs in an attempt to make it more palatable for more people? Have our members become spectators instead of worshippers, consumers who are disappointed if a service doesn't fit their taste? Are we showing proper respect for our heritage and our more conservative members?

Too many of our leaders have returned from a workshop or conference anxious to try the "latest thing" in worship with their home congregation. They have initiated change without really thinking through the emotional or theological consequences and then been surprised and disappointed by the backlash. We need to understand that it's never really been about the wallpaper. The real issue is what the wallpaper represents. The important issues in our struggle over worship are not whether it's biblical to raise one's hands or clap during a song. Much of what's happening relates directly to our positions on the interpretation of scripture, the real meaning of worship, the role of women and the use of instrumental music. Perhaps one of the reasons we have spent so much time arguing about praise teams and Power Point is that we are afraid to go into an even bigger minefield. But the future of our church depends on how we handle that discussion.[5]

Joshua 22 contains a fascinating account of a conflict over worship. Israel had conquered her enemies and taken possession of the Promised Land. Soldiers from Reuben, Gad and Manassah had left the army and headed home to their families on the far side of the Jordan. Before crossing the river, however, they built an altar. When the rest of Israel learned what their kinsmen had done, they assumed that they were planning to offer unauthorized sacrifices. Israel's leaders were angry and afraid of the consequences such an inappropriate act might have for the whole nation. So they prepared to go to war against their brothers. Before attacking they sent a delegation to confront their erring kinsmen. "How could you rebel like this?" they asked. "God will be displeased if you offer sacrifices on this altar and all his people will suffer for your sin." The leaders of Reuben, Gad and Manassah re-sponded with great conviction, "The Mighty One, God, the Lord! He knows! And let Israel know!" They explained that the altar was not meant for sacrifices at all but as a "witness" between the tribes on both sides of the Jordan that they shared allegiance to the same God. It was a symbol of their devotion to the Almighty and to each other. "Far be it from us to rebel against the Lord," they concluded. When the leaders of Israel heard this, they accepted what their brothers had done and rejoiced. "They were glad to hear the report and praised God. And they talked no more about going to war against them" (Josh. 22:33).

The current tension over worship does not have to escalate into a "war." Instead, this could be a time of positive worship revival in all of our churches. Whatever our preferences and practices may be, we share allegiance to the same God. None of us are trying to rebel against the Lord. Let's show love and respect to one another. Let's be willing to ask the tough questions together. And in everything we do let's give honor to the God we worship.

Notes

1. David Di Sabatino, "The Ongoing Impact of Revival," *Worship Leader*, July/August 1999, 23.

2. LaMar Boschman, *Future Worship* (Ventura, CA: Renew Books, 1999), 122.

3. Robert Webber, *Signs and Wonders* (Nashville: Abbott Martyn, 1992), 22-23, 26.

4. George Barna, *The Barna Report 1994-95: Virtual America* (Ventura, CA: Regal Books, 1994), 59.

5. For an indepth treatment of worship, with an eye to current issues and tensions among Churches of Christ, see Perry C. Cotham, *Ceasefire: Ending Worship Wars through Sound Theology and Plain Common Sense* (Orange, CA: New Leaf, 2001).

5

The War Is Over

Milton Jones

The Confederate flag was still flying. The Civil War was over. The heights of the Civil Rights movement were history. But the flag was still flying. And it was the day we were to remember Martin Luther King, Jr.

As I watched the protests over the Confederate flag flying over South Carolina and Georgia, emotions were rising among all the people gathered. Two camps had emerged. As the television broadcasters asked the people for their viewpoints, I couldn't help myself. I leaped to another time. I found myself in another issue. But I understood.

For one group of Southerners, the Confederate flag represented their heritage. It was a symbol of their history, their roots. It told them who they were, and they didn't want to forget. To remove the flag was to lose their past and its traditions.

But for the others, no sign symbolized oppression more. It brought back the shame of slavery. The past did not conjure up sweet memories. And it was next to impossible to get past the past with the symbol of the hurt still flying. To move forward in hope and healing, the flag needed to come down.

Who was more emotional? It was hard to tell. Who was correct? Your answer may depend on where you live or the color of your skin. At least that appears to be the cause on the surface. But on another level, it may have everything to do with justice. And it was all on a day when we were thinking of Martin Luther King, Jr.

The Flag Still Flies

As I made my quantum leap to another place and issue, I was in church. And my issue was one that emerged as a controversy right after the Civil War. Many denominations openly split between North and South after the War. Mine didn't. At least, it wasn't a division with regional clarity. Certainly, it was pretty much a North and South separation—at least it ended up that way. But it wasn't over the issues that divided the nation. No, the division that put brother against brother was over the issue of instrumental music in worship services. And it was emotional too.

Now we are past the nineteenth and even the twentieth centuries. The new millennium has emerged. But the emotions are still there. And so is the issue. For me and others like me, the exclusively a cappella position of Churches of Christ is like the flag flying. It is the sign. Two sides emerge when it is mentioned. And it is rarely mentioned anymore simply because we don't like the emotions that it arouses.

For one group a cappella music represents their heritage more than any other sign. It is the distinctive that makes their group readily recognizable. It marks their heritage. It tells their history. The songs bring back the memories of the past. The style of music tells us who we are. To change would be to lose the past with its traditions that have been cherished through the years.

But for others it is the sign that we are still in the past. Many have been hurt in this particular heritage. It was done through legalism, judgmentalism and exclusivism. Maybe it could be called religious manipulation, but many would honestly say it was more like spiritual slavery. And they want to find healing. They want to move forward. But this one position is like the flag that flies symbolizing that we must stay the same.

Why won't the ones who want a cappella music change? It is more than heritage for many. It is conviction. Even if nearly all of Christendom doesn't agree, they must be faithful. To give up the cause is to lose all for which they have been fighting. They lose identity. How would they be recognized? What would our ancestors think?

Why won't the ones who want instrumental music just leave? Because it is their heritage too. It is like the dysfunctional family. You may get beat up, but you still want to go home. It is your home, and you just want it to be well.

I wish it was just the Civil War. I wish it was merely the time after the war. I wish it would have ended quickly after we recognized a division in 1906. But I preach for a congregation that was started around 1906. And I preach for a church that is in the North. And the music hasn't died. And the flag is still flying. And the emotions are still here.

A Predicament

The last three decades have seen an explosion of contemporary Christian music. It has practically defined the movement of the message of Christ in post-baby boomer generations. It has been the heart and soul of many growing churches and movements. Young people flock to the music and are touched by the emotion of the spiritual experience.

But for our young people, it happened on the outside. They had to go someplace else to get it. Most often without blessing, they went to hear and worship in a new way. They brought the music home to their bedrooms. It became more acceptable in youth groups. In fact, the music became the dominating factor of Christian influence not just outside Churches of Christ but in our own circles. It permeated everything but the organized church itself. As a result, a couple of generations, who felt as if music was their soul, finally had their soul touched by God. It happened every place but at church.

We had ended up in a predicament. Church became the one place where what was touching their soul spiritually was forbidden. Certainly it was a generational issue too. Before the music revolution of the 60s, music was viewed as entertainment. But when the social revolution of the 60s took place, the spokespeople of the day were not politicians or preachers. They were musicians. During and after this age, music was not merely for entertainment. It was the place people turned to get their worldview. Certainly a secular worldview was being presented. But good could still overcome evil—and the contemporary Christian music scene was born. The worldview of Christ was penetrating the souls of people all over the globe through music.

And this is what the young people where I preach wanted. They didn't want the message that penetrated their souls not to penetrate their church. They wanted some of the same music that they listened to six days a week to be there on the seventh. Could it happen?

It's hard to take a flag down and leave it flying at the same time. Looking back, I think that is what we tried to do. We wondered: Could we have both? Is it possible for a church to allow freedom for both sides? Could we be one church and express ourselves to God differently but all out of equal conviction? Could we have one service where we sang a cappella for those who believe and desire to worship God with that form? And could we have an alternative assembly with instruments for the ones who wanted and needed to express praise in this way? Could we give each other the freedom to do what they believed?

That was the plan. What was the lesson? I'm probably still learning it.

We responded to the desire to have an alternative instrumental assembly with a "yes." It seemed like the godly thing to do. We already had two strong viewpoints on this issue. It didn't seem to be in the core issues of faith and salvation. In fact, it seemed to be at the core of the fellowship issue when Paul stated, "Accept one another." But could we?

Many of the young people were told by the leadership that a new assembly would be started. But because of the protests of others, it was postponed and postponed. It became obvious for some that even though they didn't have to participate in an instrumental service, they couldn't allow anyone else to do it either. If they did, they could no longer be a part of this church. Freedom was something they couldn't allow because of their convictions.

The younger people who were promised a new service and the ability to express their worship as they believed were denied their convictions. Pretty soon most all of them left. They had loved the congregation because its members had first led them to the Lord. But the church had rejected their desire and need to grow in a worship expression not understood by others in the church. They did not leave in a rage—just disappointed that they were not given freedom. They felt that their spiritual parents simply wouldn't listen. They felt that their spiritual parents cared more about their traditions than they did about them.

And thus in a short time, the church got older. The young were leaving. The church with a reputation for reaching the young now had a reputation for alienating them and not keeping promises. The major method of touching the young—contemporary Christian music—had been denied.

Why It Matters

This may seem like an isolated event, but it will be a critical reason for our lack of evangelism in the future. Paul Tans, in his insightful book on trends, *Signs of the Times*, reveals that 95% of Americans who become Christians do so before the age of 25. If that is not staggering enough, Thom Ranier, in his book, *Closing the Back Door*, states that in America 82% of the people who become Christians do so before the age of 20. It just keeps getting younger and younger. And if that wasn't enough, he expanded his study and found that 75% of Americans who become Christians do so between the ages of 9 and 14. In other words, if you don't reach Americans when they are very young, you will miss them with the gospel. And if contemporary Christian music is where they best hear the gospel, Churches of Christ may have eclipsed the message from most young people.

Why are our churches not evangelistic like they used to be? The answer is simple. We are not reaching the young. Why aren't we reaching the young? We are not speaking in a way in which they hear.

Perhaps the second biggest sociological shift in the history of the world took place in the 90s. Two cultural and philosophical changes occurred that will radically alter the church whether we like it or not.

The first is postmodernism. In postmodernism truth is seen as a multiple choice rather than the unique end of a valid syllogism. Postmodernism produced great difficulties for Churches of Christ who were born out of and operated well in a modern world. Our approaches to evangelism and discovering doctrine were always well worked out in a logical, rational and linear method. We would tell you "the truth."

Today's postmodern world does not want anyone telling them "the truth." In fact, they don't believe that there is a "truth." Still, as Christians we believe that there is "truth." As a result, the truth must somehow be revealed in our evangelistic efforts. However, in a postmodern world, if "the truth" is ever reached, it will be through discovery rather than leading a person through a bunch of prescribed and ordered steps.

In a postmodern world, truth is discovered through experience. This does not set well with modern Churches of Christ. Our answer would be that experience doesn't define truth. That is correct, but the goal of a Christian in a postmodern world is to get the lost to discover "the truth" through experience. Perhaps no method is better for a postmodern world than discovering and experiencing "the truth" through music.

The second problem for us is post-denominationalism. Most of the big doctrinal conflicts that have been fought over for centuries are no longer being fought over. If you are looking for a church that is proclaiming "just follow the Bible," you can find them all over the place. We are not unique in that plea any more. Years ago people in Churches of Christ did not know what was out there in other churches. That is not true today. And it is not only true of our people, it is also true of the unchurched. They know what is out there.

What we must realize is that people in the pews and the ones who have not even come in the door are pretty much like "free agents" in the sports world. They don't have much loyalty to their long-term team. They will quickly go somewhere else. Many who at one time would always be "Church of Christ" are finding themselves attracted to other places. And they are not leaving because they want doctrinal laxity. No, they are moving because they want freedom. They want to experience God in worship. They want the flag to come down.

The War Is Over

Taking Down the Flag

Well, after the young left our church, we decided to do something. We would start an alternative service after all. That's when we started losing on the other side. Those that could not allow the freedom for instrumental music began to leave.

We had tried to love everybody. But it seemed to be impossible. We had tried to have a church where everyone could practice their faith according to their own conviction on an issue that was not at the core of Christian doctrine—but it was like someone was putting up the flag as fast as another could take it down.

Finally, the elders asked me to speak on the subject. I gave a presentation of the instrumental music controversy for 90 minutes one memorable Sunday night. The church was packed—standing room only. To the best of my ability, I tried to be fair to both sides. But most of the young people who had left were already long gone. Most of the people who were opposed refused even to hear that there could be another side. They wanted to hear Bible, but they weren't open to the possibility that they could have been wrong. My talk on the music controversy tracked through hermeneutical arguments, biblical passages, historical reasons, theological issues and analysis of what led to the division of 1906.

When I started there was so much tension in the room that you could hardly breathe. You could hear a pin drop. I told an opening joke. No one laughed. After 90 minutes of indepth analysis, I was tired and frustrated that we had turned a fringe matter of faith into a pivotal issue. I didn't know how to end it all. So I just stopped and sat down on the front pew. There was a brief silence. Then the applause came. It was a roar. And it didn't stop. People just kept clapping. And it just wouldn't stop. Someone had come out of the closet. We had dared to talk about what we couldn't talk about. There was actually freedom to say what you believed even if it didn't exactly own up to your heritage. Smiles abounded (with most). You could breathe again. People talked. There was fellowship again at church.

But more people left. They couldn't quite handle the freedom. The next day someone put my name on some website and people emailed from all over the country to tell me I had a demon. One even sent my computer a virus. I'm sure it was sent in love. But there is always a cost to freedom.

I know some would say this isn't a freedom issue. They would say it is a doctrinal issue. My conclusion was that Christians today can prefer a cappella music. Christians today can also worship a cappella because it is their tradition and heritage. I admit we tend to sing better than other churches. And I even think one can say I believe a cappella music is correct because of the way I interpret the Bible.

But on the other hand, I don't think that we have enough actual Bible itself to bind our interpretation on others or hinder people from practicing another style of worship. I was always told in Sunday School as a child that if I was on a desert island by myself and someone dropped a Bible from the sky, I should be able to read it and end up with our biblical practice. It is my belief that if someone were on that island and read from Genesis to Revelation, he would not end up with our beliefs on this issue unless he had some preconceived ideas going into the study. And the problem is that many of our interpretations are rooted in methods that were born not out of the Bible itself but modernism.

I don't expect everyone to agree with me. I don't really want to leave Churches of Christ simply because I don't see eye to eye with every group on every issue. It is still my heritage and family too. I guess I have been burned by the movement and at times felt enslaved by it. Maybe I am attracted to the dysfunctional, but God seems to be too. And every group still needs preachers.

It's funny because the next Sunday after my address, we gathered for church. We sang a cappella that Sunday morning. Many said it was the best singing that we ever had in the history of our congregation. Several told me it was because it was the first time they sang a cappella not because they had to but because they wanted to. On Sunday evening we had a coffee house meeting where a worship band led us in some singing. Actually, we didn't sing as well as Sunday morning. We weren't accustomed to instruments. Some were fearful because they had never done it before. But others were in absolute tears of joy because they never thought they would actually get to experience this freedom. In fact, one member of the worship band was crying out of happiness because for 29 years he had wanted to use his gift of music and now for the first time it was happening. Freedom is scary when it is new. But freedom is absolutely transforming when it is finally realized for the first time.

The War Is Over

When it comes to change, Churches of Christ are going to have to talk about the instrumental music issue. And we have to get past some of the emotions that we carry. It is as if we are still fighting the Civil War. And if you haven't noticed, the war is over.

When it comes to change, we need to change for the sake of the mission. We don't need to change simply for the sake of change. But if we are not reaching the world and there is a way to communicate God's grace to people today, shouldn't we openly discuss it? To win the world to Christ, we are going to have to allow some freedom, and we are not going to get our way on every issue.

What is the end of my story? I don't know. We started an alternative service. And we kept two a cappella assemblies. For some of the young we were too slow in our change. They couldn't wait. They are some place else. I'm not sure young people are going to wait on Churches of Christ to change.

We hope with the changes we are currently making that we can reach another group of young people with the gospel. We also hope that our entire body can learn some lessons about freedom. And maybe some of us who are older can learn something about experiencing God from those who are younger.

Through this experience I learned that some are not going to change. I still love those who disagree with me and don't see the mission the same way I do. I would hate to think that the many years we ministered together were for nothing. No, God will not take away the fruit of our past labors. And most of those who disagree with me haven't left the Lord. They are simply in churches that reflect their own viewpoints.

But I still preach in a church. And there are still a lot of people there. And we have a reborn mission. We also have a new sense of freedom. Some of our heritage is so painful that we want to forget it. We still have trouble talking about it. But we haven't left because we think God is going to heal us. And freedom is very good. I don't think the flag is still flying here. The war is over. It's not that we don't want to remember the past. We just want to go back a little bit further in our memory—not to the nineteenth century but to the first. Not to the flag but to the cross.

Postscript
This chapter is going to press over a year after it was written. The Northwest Church now has two styles of worship that are extremely non-competitive. The new instrumental service has, in fact, reached many young people as was the hope. But it has also become surprisingly intergenerational and the largest assembly at Northwest. On the other hand, our a cappella services are also growing. The end result has been a greater love and spirit of peace among the various generations in the congregation. The Lord is blessing the whole church in its commitment to worship and freedom.

6

Beyond the Quick Fix

Phil Ware

Advertisers will use any edge they can to market their "stuff" these days. Two merely cosmetic techniques are widely practiced. One technique is to change the packaging to make the product look nicer, different and better without making any changes at all in the product itself—"Packaging is everything" the old adage goes. The other technique is really a labeling ploy and not much of a change. Make a small insignificant change in the product and then market it as "new and improved."

The Temptation of the Quick Fix

Churches can easily get caught up in a similar shell game. They make a few cosmetic changes, call it some kind of renewal, and then start a seminar to talk about how this new insight or practice has revolutionized everything. If the church grows rapidly, then their newfound change may even become a church growth fad. Sooner or later, other churches feel the pressure to initiate similar procedures or programs because they are "necessary if their church is going to grow and make an impact." These tag-a-long churches make a mad rush to read what they can and attend the proper seminars, so that they can get a better handle on this great new idea. They pursue this new concept with diminishing intensity until the next new fad rolls around, then the cycle begins again.

A friend sent me an e-mail recently that compared this brand of renewal to a "remodeled" cafe in his area. The owners had painted the place, printed new menus and hired a different manager. Everything was supposedly "new and improved." The problem was, the cook was the same, the items listed in the new menus were the same and the food was as bad as ever. It was the same bad food in a new, brighter environment. It was a change, but not a real improvement. Much of what passes for church renewal could be judged to be strikingly similar.[1]

While we would all like to believe that our church and our methods are above such silliness, we know we aren't. The passion that leads us to cross cultural barriers at great expense with the gospel, and the desire to be a congregation that impacts its community, quite often makes us vulnerable to fads, gimmicks and the latest new trend in "church renewal." Of course our own desire to please and entertain ourselves also enters into the equation and, before long, we find ourselves doing the silliest of things for the flimsiest of reasons.

So how do we pursue church growth and spiritual vitality without prostituting our church integrity on the altars of trendy fads, hokey gimmicks and simply selfish interests?

To experience God's newness, to participate in genuine spiritual renewal, we're going to have resist the quick fixes and realize that only an encounter with the Lord can give our congregations the renewal we seek. Sticking "new and improved" on lifeless predictability isn't going to make it spiritual renewal. Changing everything around us to be like some church from out of town without evaluating the reason or the methods isn't going to lead to transformation, just chaotic change. Changing the menu without changing the cook is not going to leave us with anything other than a prettier environment in which to eat the same old stuff. The Lord wants us to have genuine freshness in our congregations. So instead of distracting ourselves by changing things cosmetically, let's really pursue an encounter with the Living God.

How do we do that? While Isaiah's encounter with God in the Temple (Isaiah 6) can be a model of such an experience,[2] we have to admit that Isaiah didn't have one of those transformational experiences every Sabbath. John's great Revelation on the Lord's Day was an incredible experience, but how often did he have that kind of Sunday?[3] How do we find a set of guidelines that lets our churches experience genuine renewal in the midst of mundane ministry and the routine ups and downs of life? Surely we want to get off the treadmill of trying to pull a bigger and bigger rabbit out of our hat each Sunday so our people will go home _____ (choose your favorite word to fill in the blank: thrilled, satisfied, uplifted, motivated, encouraged, touched, moved, etc.).

On the other hand, surely we want to get out of the lifeless and lackadaisical predictability that makes church so irrelevant to so many people. Where do we find balance and authenticity in our congregations that opens them to genuine spiritual renewal?

Authentic Encounter with God

Rather than simplistically and naively trying to offer a comprehensive method or grandiose plan, let's look at one that is given to us in the structure and theology of Matthew's Gospel.

While the Gospel of Matthew is known for many things, one of Matthew's particular emphases is especially relevant to our discussion of church renewal—defined here as God's people having an authentic encounter with God, through Jesus and his work. We will call them the Immanuel sayings. Four verses stand out as the key Immanuel sayings in the Gospel of Matthew:

> 1:23 "The virgin will be with child and will give birth to a son, and they will call him Immanuel, which means, 'God with us.'"
> 18:20 "For where two or three come together in my name, there am I with them."
> 25:40 "The King will reply, 'I tell you the truth, whatever you did for one of the least of these brothers of mine, you did for me.'"
> 28:18-20 "All authority in heaven and on earth has been given to me. Therefore go and make disciples of all nations, baptiz-

ing them in the name of the Father and of the Son and of the Holy Spirit, and teaching them to obey everything I have commanded you. And surely I am with you always, to the very end of the age."

Matthew tells Jesus' story in an structured way[4] to help his readers see God entering the world to fulfill the great promises of the Old Testament[5] and bring salvation to both Jews and Gentiles.[6] As Jesus preaches, teaches and heals,[7] he is Immanuel, "God with us" (1:23). As we read this Gospel, Matthew helps us come to know Jesus and also introduces us to Immanuel, "God with us," as Jesus ministers in Galilee.

The whole tone of the Gospel shifts with Peter's confession in chapter 16. Once the disciples begin to see him as "Christ, the Son of the living God" (16:16), Jesus begins to prepare them for his death, resurrection and commission: "From that time on Jesus began to explain to his disciples that he must go to Jerusalem and suffer many things at the hands of the elders, chief priests and teachers of the law, and that he must be killed and on the third day be raised to life" (16:20). The emphasis on Jesus as "Immanuel, God with us," now shifts to his presence with his disciples after his passion and resurrection, as Matthew highlights by his use of the word "church" (16:18 and 18:17).

In cornbread English, Matthew gives us an Immanuel theology for the church. We can know and experience the presence of God with us in Jesus by knowing and seeing (hearing and reading about) his ministry (Matt. 4:17-16:20). This is clearly a call for us to re-enter the world of Jesus and open the story of his ministry expecting an encounter with God. We also can experience Immanuel in the life of our church when we share in fellowship, worship and discipline (18:20).

But more than just a focus on "worship renewal" or the reading of Scripture, Matthew calls us to a fuller view of encountering God. Immanuel is experienced in our sacrificial service to others, especially our brothers and sisters in Christ,[8] as we meet Jesus in the faces and lives of those we serve (25:34-40). Matthew leaves us with the powerful reminder that Immanuel goes with us as we go about his mission; as we cross cultural and geographical barriers to share the Gospel, baptize new believers, and mature them in obedience to Christ, we experience Immanuel, God with us in Jesus.

Implications for Spiritual Renewal

What implications do these insights have for us as we yearn for renewal in our churches and ministries today? I'm sure there are more than can be addressed in this brief treatment of the subject, but let's look at a few.

First, we must realize that renewal isn't going to happen because of a gimmick or some new program. God may choose to use something in our programming, but only an encounter with the Living God is going to produce lasting and redemptive change. After living through the decade when "worship is what happens away from the church assemblies" to the decade when "renewal is not going to happen until we make our weekly worship services user friendly," we surely have seen that the pendulum makes huge swings. Instead of looking to one area in which renewal is going to take place, let's realize, based on Matthew's model, that an encounter with Immanuel may happen for some in worship and fellowship, for others in service and benevolent care, for others in cross-cultural missions and evangelism, and for others in searching the Gospels and meeting Jesus in his story.

Second, the story of Jesus clearly needs to play a more predominant role in our lives as individuals and churches. Any movement that dares to call itself the "church of Christ" had better make sure that its life, ministry, character and values reflect the One it claims to honor. For this to happen, Jesus must be preached and the Gospels must be read. This reading, however, must transcend the mere acquisition of data about Jesus' life, teaching and ministry. We must approach the Gospels, and especially Matthew's Gospel, with an anticipation of an encounter with Immanuel, God with us. We must read, see[9] and hear this Gospel asking God to help us know Jesus and seeking God as he works through Jesus in our world.

Third, let's be careful about blueprinting our generational focus or our personality type as the one that will reach everyone. We know that at different times in our lives and because of different interests some of us are going to be especially open to meeting God through serving others. Campus and youth ministers have known this for years. Stretched beyond their capabilities, teens and young adults find it exhilarating to see Jesus use them beyond their abilities. Increasingly, older adults are going on cross-cultural mission trips and coming back convinced that God has worked through them in ways they could have never imagined; as they served to honor the Christ, they experienced Immanuel. Others find Jesus real in worship, no matter the chosen "style" in which that worship is clothed or the size of the gathering. There are still others who truly see Jesus come to life as they study his story in Scripture.

The bottom line is that we must make a commitment to pursue Immanuel in each area of experience Jesus outlined for us in the Gospel of Matthew. If we don't, someone is going to get left out because their current life circumstances makes that a hard area to pursue or because that is not their primary way of experiencing the world. Even worse, we may begin to think that there is one sure-fire way to make renewal happen and thus pursue a very unbalanced view of discipleship, leaving us open to the ever-present temptation to chase fads and think renewal is about cosmetic changes. Let's not get caught repainting the restaurant, buying new menus, and keeping the same ol' cook cooking the same ol' dinners.

God made us to seek him! Only an encounter with the Living God, through Jesus, is going to satisfy our soul's deepest longings. While it may not be flashy, new or trendy, Matthew's Immanuel sayings offer us a good place to start in evaluating our ministries and our purposes. Are we calling people to Immanuel in word, worship, service and mission? Or are we simply offering the latest fad which will quickly be exhausted and reinforce the rampant consumerism that plagues good people as they search for a meaningful experience that only knowing God can fulfill?

Notes

1. Please understand that this is not a criticism of the church growth movement or the desire for churches to grow. Neither is it a closet slam on church renewal or worship renewal. As part of a growing urban church, the author has a passionate desire to be a part of a growing and dynamic church. His frustration is with our tendency to chase fads without looking at biblical foundations for renewal and without looking at the systems dynamics of the churches that are often used as models.

2. Who can argue with the movement from "Crisis to Divine Encounter to Holy Awe to Awareness of Sin to Cleansing to Mission" found in Isaiah 6? But even Isaiah didn't have this life-changing experience every week.

3. John's experience follows remarkably the flow of Isaiah's (cf. note 2), but his apocalyptic vision is known because of its uniqueness in the New Testament not because it was expected to be the norm.

4. Two ways of recognizing Matthew's structure are commonly accepted. The oldest recognizes five blocks of ministry in word (5:1-7:27; 10:1-42; 13:1-52; 18:1-35; 23:1-25:46) separated by blocks of ministry in deed. The blocks of teaching are concluded with a statement beginning with, "When Jesus had finished" (7:28; 11:1; 13:53; 19:1; 26:1) and begin with a clear address to his disciples (5:1; 10:1; 13:1 & 10; 18:1; 23:1) The second view emphasizes the parallel "from that time on" sayings of 4:17 and 16:21; these divide Matthew into three clear sections: The Beginnings of Jesus, Son of God (1:1-4:16), The Ministry of Jesus (4:17-16:20), and The Passion and Resurrection of Jesus, Son of God (16:22-28:20). It should be emphasized that these views are not necessarily exclusive of one another, and both give increased credibility to the Immanuel thesis outlined here.

5. Matthew uses a fulfillment formula ("this was to fulfill") at least 15 times in his Gospel and pays careful attention to Jesus' connection with the Old Testament throughout his gospel story.

6. While emphasizing that Jesus' earthly ministry was to the People of Israel (10:6; 15:24), the gospel clearly anticipates a mission to all peoples. This emphasis is made clear from the beginning with the story of the Magi from the East (Matt. 2) and with his final words detailing the Great Commission (28:18-20) as well as anticipating the faith of non-jews (cf. 8:5-10).

7. This is Matthew's capsule characterization of Jesus' ministry in 4:23 and 9:35.

8. A careful reading of Matthew's Gospel, and especially the context of Matthew 25, reveals that "the least of these" are best understood as fellow believers. Luke's account of Paul's conversion says a similar thing: what is done to Christians is done to Christ (Acts 9:5). Paul's doctrine of the church as the Body of Christ is another example of this understanding in the early church.

9. The availability of the Gospel of Matthew, word for word on video, has opened a new horizon with both blessings and limitations. But we need to be aware that this video presentation of the gospel may be a primary means for many people to become acquainted with Matthew's story of Jesus.

7

Facing Our True Selves: Becoming Voices of Courage in a New Age

Paul Casner

There is no fear in love, but perfect love casts out fear" (1 John 4:18).

An Age of Fear

In the so-called "postmodern" age, our culture's old standards of right and wrong have crumbled. We no longer have tried and true cultural norms on which to rely for making our way in the world, and this threatens our sense of identity. We are not as sure as we once were who we are, what we are to do, or where we are going. As a result, we live in an age of fear.

Different segments of our society have chosen to deal with this fear in various ways. Some people find security in their career or their possessions. Others rely on local militias or religious cults. Many well-intentioned Christian groups preach that we can only find security if we get "back to the basics" of a particular ethical code, a specific political party, even a single church.

All of these are misguided attempts to find security in today's uncertain world. One of the greatest temptations we face in Churches of Christ at this time is to follow our culture in embracing these routes to security. We are especially susceptible in this regard in light of our past. In the twentieth century, Churches of Christ have tended to be easy targets for quick fixes to fear. In fact, many of the beliefs and practices of Churches of Christ in the twentieth century can be explained as flawed attempts to deal with fear.

A People of Fear

For example, we have often emphasized that we are the only legitimate church.[1] The evidence we offered for this, in many quarters, was our superior knowledge of the Bible. We tended to believe that we knew the Bible better than other groups, therefore we were in a position to obey God better than them. Other denominations, in our estimation, knew that Bible study was the key to legitimate obedience but failed to dedicate themselves sufficiently to that task. This signified, in our view, a moral defect in them. They rebelled against God because they refused to work hard enough to "rightly divide" the scriptures. Because of this, God would in all likelihood condemn them at the day of judgment.

While not everyone bought all of this in Churches of Christ, such attitudes helped provide us with a clear sense of identity. We knew who we were and where we were going. Moreover, we knew what we should be doing—converting other professing Christians to our point of view.

Such a theology is tailor-made for a people living in changing times. It has been well documented that Churches of Christ, at the beginning of our century, were a "wrong side of the tracks" group. Our identity was greatly influenced by the cultural upheaval of the South in reconstruction days. The old order, with its tried and true standards of value and class, was "gone with the wind," and with it went its clear answers to questions of human worth and place. Thus we entered the twentieth century searching for an identity that would sustain us in this new world. Events of the twentieth century—depression, war, cold war and social upheaval—served to aggravate our need for certainty and direction. It is no coincidence that the culture which produced Joseph McCarthy and bomb shelters was the context in which Churches of Christ refined and hardened their sectarian stance.[2]

Churches of Christ formulated a theology of certainty, offering "black and white" answers to difficult questions, in part to deal with the fear of living in such times. We found a way to assure ourselves that we were the only true people of God because we lived in a world which threatened our security. We have been a very frightened people.

Courage to Face Our True Selves

In spite of the fears stimulated in Churches of Christ by uncertain times, the most fundamental fear we faced was fear of ourselves. Any good Alfred Hitchcock movie teaches us that the most frightening things we face in life are not so much the dangers that threaten us from outside but those that threaten from inside. The gospel of Jesus Christ brings us to this same recognition. It is not, as Jesus said, what goes into a person that defiles a person. Rather, it is what comes out that corrupts. And when the light that is within us is darkness, how great is that darkness (Mk. 7:17-23; Matt. 6:23). To come face to face with the reality of our sin is our greatest fear, because the recognition of sin leads us to question our worth. To see oneself as unworthy of love is the most terrifying vision a person can have.

I believe it is this kind of fear that, at root, has gripped twentieth-century Churches of Christ. We have been terribly frightened of facing our true selves. Deep down, often unconsciously, we realized that we did not measure up to God's standards. This was a terrifying realization because God, in our view, would not save people who did not measure up. The frontier culture in which we lived in the early days of our movement taught us that. If a people did not know how to take care of themselves on the frontier, they were finished. The "social Darwinism" of the latter nineteenth and early twentieth centuries made a similar point: only the fittest survive. The increasingly competitive world of the depression, World War II and the cold war solidified these beliefs in our mind.

Encountering flaws in our inmost selves was a terrifying thing. It meant we were not "fit" for spiritual survival. As a people we constantly faced a fearful, even hopeless existence. In order to avoid the pain of facing such an existence, we tended to suppress awareness of our true sinfulness and live in a world founded on delusion. We emphasized certain aspects of God's law that we felt we could perform reasonably well. This list of beliefs was viewed as the essence of the Gospel, and exalted to a preeminent position among God's commands. These commands, and our superior obedience to them, served to make fear of our sinful selves manageable. The feeling of control this approach gave us enabled us to feel as if we had a final say in who we were and what would happen to us in the uncertain world in which we lived.

In his fine book, *The Core Gospel*, Bill Love points out that he has met "scores of people over the years" in Churches of Christ "who wonder if God loves them and what they might do to win his favor." According to Love, this fundamental anxiety about salvation has made many of us in Churches of Christ susceptible to all kinds of faddish means for attaining religious security. In Love's words, we have tended to migrate from a "salvation by legalism" to a "salvation by knowledge"; from "salvation by social activism" to "salvation by religious experience or feelings."[3] We have often been hardened in our "official" positions about who is saved and why because we are deeply anxious about our own status before God.

The key flaw in all of this is an inadequate view of God's grace. We have allowed our inner fears, in combination with the fears that pervaded our culture, to lead us to embrace a god who saves only those fit for survival—those who meet certain standards of obedience in order to qualify for entrance into God's loving embrace.

This god is not the God of Jesus Christ. The Christian God accepts people "while they are still sinners" (Rom. 5:8). In the cross and resurrection of Jesus Christ, God reconciles people to himself in an ultimate sense while they are still rebelling against him—before any acts of repentance or obedience have taken place (Rom. 5:10). Sinners are enabled to desire to love God and others because God's love has awakened love in their hearts. Thus we read in I John 4:19, "We love because he first loved us." Similarly Paul struggles to obey God not in order to get God to accept him but "because Christ Jesus has made me his own" (Phil. 3:12).

These beliefs are not novel. Many mainstream Christian traditions have for centuries dealt with fear by relying on this message of Christ's acceptance. We find it in Augustine and his followers, in Thomas Aquinas as well as the Reformation theologies of Luther, Calvin and Zwingli. Today this message is represented by Protestant theologians like Karl Barth and Jürgen Moltmann as well as Catholic theologians like Hans Küng.[4]

Unfortunately, Churches of Christ have had trouble embracing belief in the God of grace. This has been, I believe, our most fundamental problem. It lies at the root of our fears and therefore at the root of our flawed beliefs and actions in the nineteenth and twentieth centuries. If we do not address this problem we will repeat the errors of our spiritual ancestors in Churches of Christ *ad infinitum*. We will continue to be a people enslaved by fear because we have not yet acknowledged the perfect love which casts out fear (1 John 4:18).

But what about obedience? Doesn't it have an important role to play in the Christian life? Of course. But obedience only makes sense from a Christian perspective if it occurs within the context of our acknowledgment of God's prior acceptance of us in Christ, not as a means to procure that acceptance. We obey because we have been saved, not in order to get saved. In failing to recognize this fact, we have transformed the burden of salvation away from the cross of Christ and onto our own shoulders. This is a burden we are not able to bear. So, when confronted with the depth of our sin, we recoil in terror and resort to living in delusions of security, as I have outlined.

In this regard some so-called "secular" organizations have understood the Gospel better than many Churches of Christ. For example, twelve-step programs insist that a person who is attempting to address a problem such as alcoholism, drug addiction or abusive behavior begin by admitting powerlessness in the face of their challenge. The addicted person must face up to her failure as the first step toward healing. Once this is done, she is taught to place faith in a "higher power" to enable her to begin a new life. This approach has been so successful that it has spread into a vast network of programs across the country and the world. Often, these programs meet in churches and their numbers exceed Sunday morning worship attendance.

Churches of Christ need to learn from twelve-step programs' use of Christian principles. You might say that Churches of Christ are in denial about our true state and healing cannot come unless we face what we fear most, our powerlessness before sin. Only then can we put ourselves in a position to be molded into a healthy movement by the grace of God.

But the power to face sin in spite of our fears can only come when we acknowledge God's graceful embrace of us. Then will we be free to look at our sinful state without recoiling from it. We can thus dedicate ourselves each day to battling sin without the task overwhelming us. We are freed by Christ to strive for perfection (Matt. 5:48) because our salvation does not depend on reaching perfection.

Passages in the Bible which speak of "reaping what we sow" and of the wages of sin should therefore be read within the context of the acceptance we have received in Christ, not as a means by which to obtain that acceptance. The difference between the sheep and the goats is not so much the quality of their obedience, but the recognition of Who loves them and how much he loves them (Matt. 7:24-25). It is only when we read God's commands in light of the grace we receive in Jesus Christ that we can face both the commands and ourselves honestly. Any other approach leaves us either minimizing the extent of God's law or being crushed by its demands.

In the last 15 or 20 years, we in Churches of Christ have made a lot of headway in acknowledging God's grace. But as our culture progresses in its transition from modernism to postmodernism—and as we face the fears associated with this change—we are in danger of reversing that trend. For the swirling waters of postmodernity are challenging us to rely on something less risky than God's gracious love. Love points us toward a courage which comes at God's initiation. We cannot keep this courage in our pocket and pull it out whenever we face a trying time. We can only come to God in prayer and ask for it. We must trust that God will give it to us as he has promised.

Voices of today offer the security of party, creed and physical force. They point out that Moses has been on the mountain too long, and that we do not know when or if he will come back. They then suggest the golden calf as an alternative. Because of our history, our movement today is especially susceptible to golden calves. We are at risk of following various cultural trends, embracing the easy security they offer, instead of placing the love of Jesus at the center.

But if we are willing to take the risk of love and place our well being in the hands of the One who promises that he accepted us at the cross of Christ, we can find a freedom from fear which is far greater than that offered by anything else. For it enables us to look at ourselves as we really are and accept ourselves in spite of our flaws.

Courage to Face Others

Other Christians
Accepting ourselves in this way can give us courage to face other challenges which we have often failed to meet in Churches of Christ. For example, it can help us learn to overcome our sectarianism. When you feel you must conform to a specific list of criteria to be accepted by God, you expect others to do the same. But experiencing mercy in Christ can open us to showing mercy to other Christians (Matt. 18:23-35). We may still disagree with some of their beliefs, but we can accept them as Christians anyway—just as Christ accepted us while we were still sinners. Paul says, "Welcome one another, therefore, just as Christ has welcomed you, for the glory of God" (Rom. 15:7). Embracing the God of grace in Christ can give us the courage to be a leader in ecumenical activity in the new millennium.

Other Races
Acknowledging the God of grace frees us, furthermore, to accept people of minority races and backgrounds. The recent apology by the president of Abilene Christian University for its past failures in racial matters serves to remind us that we as a movement have some sins to face on this issue. Little has been written on this, perhaps because it is so painful to face such failures. Yet the God of Jesus Christ makes clear that he accepted us not only after such an apology but at the cross. It is only when we recognize this acceptance that we can move toward a

future in which African-Americans, Caucasians, Hispanics and others can worship and work together in love in Churches of Christ.

Women
As the love of Christ frees us to accept those of different races, it also frees us to accept women alongside men. For Christ's love does not value people on the basis of sex any more than it assesses value on the basis of race or good works performed (Gal. 3:28). This recognition summons us to allow an equal role for women in the church. God calls us to a future in which our little girls and little boys learn that men and women are loved alike in God's eyes. Our children cannot learn this lesson fully until they see men and women serving alongside one another in all aspects of church life. Passages in the New Testament which seem to limit a woman's role should be read within the context of the larger biblical principle of the equality of men and women in Christ, not vice versa. Jesus addressed controversial questions in light of the "weightier matters of the law" (Matt. 23:23). We should do the same.

Courage to Face the Past

Acknowledging the grace we have received in Christ can help us show grace to our forebears in Churches of Christ. In this essay I have listed some key mistakes I believe Churches of Christ have made. It is important for us to acknowledge these mistakes in order that we might not repeat them. But this does not mean we should look down on our ancestors as somehow unacceptable to God. Nor should we think that we will completely avoid repeating their mistakes.

For, in spite of their mistakes, our forebears in Churches of Christ witnessed effectively to God in this world. This witness did not occur, of course, in the way they often understood it to occur. They were not saved because of their biblical knowledge, superior obedience or key insights. Rather they were saved because God gracefully saves those who are weak (Rom. 14:4). God's power has always been most manifest in human weakness (2 Cor. 12:1-10). That is why the symbol of God's victory over sin in this world is a cross. In all of their weakness, Churches of Christ are a living illustration of this. Their story is an important reminder to us—as well as to the rest of the world—that we should not take pride in our accomplishments but rather focus on the love of Christ.

It is an honorable calling to exhibit human weakness in service to Jesus Christ. No less a Christian than the Apostle Paul characterized his ministry in this manner (2 Cor. 11:16-12:10). What Paul recognized is that we all, ultimately, serve Christ in this way. I believe our ancestors in Churches of Christ are in heaven right now, proud to have been a part of this service. We, therefore, have no right to look down on the brothers and sisters who have come before us. Nor should we be ashamed of their story. We must learn to tell that story with its noble and less than noble moments.

Courage to Face the Future

By accepting ourselves through God's grace in Christ we can therefore find courage for the future. God's mandate to Churches of Christ in the twenty-first century is to be a voice of courage in an age characterized by fear. He calls us to do this first by acknowledging the loving embrace he gives us at the cross of Christ. Having done this, we can learn to look at ourselves in the mirror, warts and all, and love ourselves. In time, this will enable us to love God and others also.

If we can learn to do these things we will be ready for the new age, whatever it may bring.

Notes

1. C. Leonard Allen, Richard T. Hughes, & Michael R. Weed, *The Worldly Church: A Call for Biblical Renewal* (Abilene, TX: ACU Press, 1988), 1-10.

2. Richard T. Hughes, *Reviving the Ancient Faith: The Story of Churches of Christ in America* (Grand Rapids, MI: Eerdmans, 1996), 114-116, 130-131.

3. Bill Love, *The Core Gospel* (Abilene, TX: ACU Press, 1989).

4. On Augustine see Jaroslav Pelikan, *The Christian Tradition: A History of the Development of Doctrine*, Vol. 1, *The Emergence of the Catholic Tradition*

(100-600) (Chicago: University of Chicago, 1971), 292-298; on Aquinas see Arvin Vos, *Aquinas, Calvin, and Contemporary Protestant Thought.:A Critique of Protestant Views on the Thought of Thomas Aquinas* (Grand Rapids: Eerdmans, 1985), 153ff; on Luther, see Pelikan, *The Christian Tradition*, Vol. 4, *Reformation of Church and Dogma (1300-1700)* (Chicago: University of Chicago, 1984), 127-150. On the last page of this reference, Pelikan offers a noteworthy quote from Luther's 1535 *Commentary on Galatians* 4:6, "This is the reason why our theology is certain: it snatches us away from ourselves...so that we do not depend on our own strength, conscience, experience, person, or works, but depend on...the promise and truth of God, which cannot deceive." John Calvin, *The Institutes of the Christian Religion*, ed., John T. McNiell, trans. Ford Lewis Battles (Philadelphia: Westminster, 1960), 2.16.3. Here we see Calvin also speaking aptly concerning our topic, "If, then, we would be assured that God is pleased with and kindly disposed toward us, we must fix our eyes and minds on Christ alone. For actually, through him alone we escape the imputation of our sins to us...." On Calvin and Zwingli, see John T. McNiell, *The History and Character of Calvinism* (New York: Oxford University Press, 1954), 76-77, 210-212; Karl Barth, *Church Dogmatics* III/3, ed. G. W. Bromiley and T. F. Torrance, trans. G. W. Bromiley and R. J. Ehrlich (Edinburgh: T. & T. Clark, 1960), 70-73; Barth, *Church Dogmatics* IV/1, ed. G. W. Bromiley and T. F. Torrance, trans. G. W. Bromiley (Edinburgh: T. & T. Clark, 1956), 273; Hans Kung, *On Being a Christian*, trans. Edward Quinn (New York: Doubleday, 1976), 405-410; Jurgen Moltmann, *The Trinity and the Kingdom*, trans. Margaret Kohl (Minneapolis: Fortress, 1993), 57-60, 114-122.

5. Thomas H. Olbricht, *His Love Compells: The Sacrificial Message of God from the New Testament* (Joplin, MO: College Press, 2000), 189.

6. Ibid., 190-197.

———————————— Culture

8

A Final Farewell to the Twelfth Century

Dale Pauls

In all the celebrations that marked our new millennium no one noticed or mourned the death of the worldview long dominant. Neoplatonism with its dualistic, polarizing and hierarchical instincts has finally, after a reign of almost two thousand years, been consigned to the cultural trash heap of the postmodern West. Platonic thought as modified in late antiquity (the third through the fifth centuries AD) no longer dictates how we see and structure the world in which we live. Its passion for what is absolutist and perfectionist has given way to standards more humane and egalitarian.

Although long past its prime and in serious decline since the American Declaration of Independence, its death came suddenly. It crumpled finally beneath the imponderables of quantum physics, ecology, psychoanalysis and biomedical ethics. In the words of the distinguished historian Richard Southern, "It often happens at critical moments in history that ideas which have long held the field almost unchallenged are suddenly discovered, not to be wrong, but to be useless; then almost everyone can see they are absurd."[1] As a consequence of the collapse of Neoplatonism, it is no longer assumed that everyone and everything has his, her or its exact place in the way things ought to be in one great hierarchical chain of being. Rights and privileges on the basis of birth—race, gender and class—no longer seem pre-ordained.

More specifically, the twelfth century—when Neoplatonic culture reached its zenith—is at long last ending. Those were the days when, as a direct result of the Gregorian Reform of the church (whereby the papacy arrogated to itself all power it possibly could), women suffered their greatest loss in relative status and were driven to the far sidelines of church and society.[2] Those were also the days when the Western legal tradition was formed and even the church, especially the church, turned to law as its presiding metaphor and paradigm. Under a dynasty of ambitious lawyer popes, that is, popes rigorously trained in canon (or church) law, gospel was reduced to a law code and Jesus became mostly a slogan, a militant banner, a verbal formula in syllogisms leading elsewhere. In the same legal spirit, the medieval papacy forcefully defined the basis for church unity as exact uniformity when Pope Innocent III at the Fourth Lateran Council in AD 1215 insisted that only those churches exactly like the Church of Rome in faith and practice could be in fellowship with the Church of Rome. These twelfth-century patterns then proved to have tremendous staying power because they were coded into law and came to be experienced over centuries as the way things had always been and, it was assumed, always should be. As a consequence, what many people today believe to be timeless truths are, in reality, twelfth-century cultural constructs with all the limitations inherent in that time.

A Century of Extraordinary Spiritual Adventure

The challenge for a church that would be Christ's is to understand the present times and not hold on nostalgically to a world that is passing away. On one level, this means that women's voices must be heard and respected within the church; anything less than this is widely understood as discriminatory and therefore morally reprehensible. On another level, the church must realize that law no longer possesses in popular imagination the ring of absolute truth. Law is widely perceived today as a hodgepodge of *ad hoc* decisions and conflicting rules that are geared to expediency and not necessarily morality.³ This represents an enormous challenge to churches that still understand and present their message primarily in terms of law rather than gospel. Consequently, it becomes especially urgent that we return to a close reading of scripture so that we might interpret it in ways that are true to its original intent and not to the spirit of either twelfth-century canon law or eighteenth-century American constitutional law.

Having said all this, however, there is perhaps no larger problem confronting Christianity today than the relative absence of men in the historic church.⁴ Nor is this a recent trend; decline in male membership in churches is 800 years old and goes back, it seems, to the same twelfth century when women were being marginalized. Perhaps there was something about suppressing women that made men feel not stronger in the church but actually weaker. Or maybe it's just that in the twelfth century the church turned rigorously authoritarian. The papacy turned to the ways of force—to imposing church leadership by celibate men—and perhaps women found this easier to accept than men because they were more used to being submissive.

In any case, one of the next great projects for the church worldwide will be to win men back to active Christian faith by reaffirming values that have traditionally been labeled masculine and too often dismissed. The church can no longer cede to corporate America all elements of risk, sacrifice and daunting obstacles. There is a hunger in the human soul to seek out danger, to prove oneself against great odds, to take risks so that others might be saved, and to undergo costly initiation. It is time, past time, for the church to quit promising comfortable status and start offering significant task, and when this is done men and women will be drawn to the message and mission of the church.

This will be none too soon, because a century of extraordinary spiritual adventure is upon us. We now live in a global marketplace of ideas, and the truth claims of Christianity will be tested against those of Islam, Judaism, Hinduism, Buddhism, Taoism and various other world faiths. What we will find in this age of breathtaking change and astonishing diversity is a great paradox—Jesus is, in the deepest sense, the way and the truth and the life (John 14:6). It is

Jesus who tells us to love even our enemies. It is Jesus who tells us to applaud those whose faith exceeds our own whatever their heritage may be; it is Jesus who warns us that we will find faith in places and people we least expect it. It is Jesus who tells us to fraternize with those rejected by others as "sinners"; he tells us to take seriously and not to ostracize the outcasts in our society. It is Jesus who tells us to forgive those who wrong us. It is Jesus who tells us to resist those who are perfectly scrupulous in minor religious matters but neglect the more important matters of justice, mercy and integrity. It is Jesus who calls us to a ministry of reconciliation that can bring an end to centuries of ethnic and religion-driven hatred. Now it is more urgent than ever that we recover from the life, death and resurrection of Jesus his truths—truths that encourage trust, forgiveness and love for our neighbors, even our enemies; truths that promote sweet reasonableness in the face of life's undeniable complexity, ambiguity and paradox; truths that ease our fears and teach us disciplined civility in response to our differences and that nurture us to draw strength from change and cultural diversity.

Knowledge over Love

The Churches of Christ with their strong "grassroots" tradition are ideally prepared for challenges that require such diversity and flexibility. Our message, moreover, is one needed by everyone everywhere—the good news that whoever you are and whatever you have done you can start over, be reborn, be forgiven and then discover within yourself the Spirit of God. Yet, sadly, just when the entire world needs and is receptive to God's good news, all is not well in the Churches of Christ; news from everywhere tells of confusion, frustrations, losses—large losses—by attrition, and a movement in strong centrifugal spin. History—too long ignored and dismissed as irrelevant—is taking its revenge on us.

It began in this way. In the years during and immediately following the American Revolution, it was hard not to feel that we Americans were part of something grand and cosmic. We were engaged in nothing less than the establishment of a *novus ordo seclorum*—a new order of the ages—on a clean and pure virgin continent. In the words of Thomas Paine, it was "as if we had lived in the beginning of time." The glorious Enlightenment that had been imagined in Europe by thinkers such as Locke, Montesquieu and Rousseau was now being realized in America.5

We could start over. We could break free of the past and create a new society—a new Eden—uncontaminated by the traditions, corruption and mistakes, that is, the sins of Europe. Here finally things could be done perfectly. We could get it right. Religiously we could step out of history back into the church at first, the church envisioned by Jesus and established by his apostles. Once again we could live its life and breathe in its spirit. It was—and it still is—an exhilarating quest.

There were problems, however. We had trashed history. We had exempted ourselves from the centuries-long story of faith. We supposed that all chapters that came before ours were not worth reading—that the only story that mattered was our own. Believing ourselves to have escaped history, we now underestimate the hold of history on our own interpretations and applications of scripture. More problematically, having dismissed historical consciousness, we are left vulnerable to a perfectionism that dismisses the real human condition with all its ambiguities, flaws and inherent contradictions. As a result, we are much better at defining abstract and universal truths than identifying those truths necessary for living real life down on street level where things are more complicated and messier. Furthermore, we have always found it unexpectedly difficult to agree upon precisely what it is that is to be restored from the church at first. Essentially, as obedient children of the Enlightenment, we are confronted by one of the central paradoxes of the Enlightenment: how people who have learned to think for themselves (that is, people liberated from creed, cult and tradition) might be led to think identically. It is only now—as more and more people really are thinking for themselves—that we can see how large this conundrum is.

This all turns on the way in which the church fundamentally understands itself: primarily as the depository of knowledge rather than love. In spite of the warnings of Paul and John (1 Cor. 8-10; 1, 2 & 3 John), *gnosis* (Greek for knowledge) is now woven into the fabric of the church. It is at the core of how the church—every church—understands itself. From Hellenistic thinkers, we acquired a passion for definition (hence Nicaea). Following the Latin legal tradition, we transformed gospel into church law. From the medieval papacy, we learned to define unity as uniformity and to accept in fellowship only those who are exactly like us in thought and practice. With the spread of the printing press in the fifteenth century, doctrinal lines that had previously been crossed and recrossed without anyone hardly noticing became drawn in indelible black ink; from then on, orthodoxy could be easily standardized and any deviation from it quickly detected. Then from seventeenth-century scientists, we learned to accept as truth only what was logical, exact, certain, quantified, categorized and verifiable. Century by century it has increasingly become for everyone knowledge, knowledge, knowledge to the virtual exclusion (or at least marginalization) of lifestyle, trust and love. Religious faith now resides in certainty for certainty's sake, so that certainty itself becomes the hermeneutics—even if the facts must be stretched and real life twisted to fit it. The result is that all too often there is something terribly hard about church people—a ferocious, alienating certainty, a look in the eyes when the mind has stopped considering variables.

This is the truth. A community built upon gospel must be a community built upon grace. The church Jesus gives us is a welcoming gathering place, unpretentious, warm, informal, with an at-home atmosphere. Common meals are shared in the memory and name of Jesus. Status doesn't matter—at all! All can feel free to share their doubts and fears and failures, and their joys and triumphs. All drawn to faith can feel accepted and treasured for themselves. Evenings are filled with conversation and camaraderie as we learn to face struggle and hardship together, always celebrating the great good news of our Father God who welcomes outcasts and sinners.

If, however, we learn to think for ourselves—that is, if we are truly freed from creed and cult—we cannot be expected to think identically. Common sense tells us this. Scripture confirms it (Rom. 14:1-15:13; 1 Cor. 8-10). History insists on it, and history disregarded will avenge itself.

A Final Farewell to the Twelfth Century

Restorationist Longings

Fortunately we are learning these lessons, and just in time. We live in times that will be remembered and talked and written about, maybe for a thousand years. The things we decide and do now will have lasting consequences. This is true for our churches, our nation and our little planet Earth. This is partly because we stand at the birth of a new millennium, but there is more. The generation that represents our future—the twentysomethings—is unlike those who have come before. And the generations following them will be like them, only more so. They are the first generations of many to come of age in an America characterized by astonishing religious and cultural pluralism. A Christian in college today may have a Muslim roommate and a Hindu lab partner; his or her closest friend may be Nigerian or Vietnamese.

For this reason and many others, those now moving into adulthood—and those coming after—face far more life choices than previous generations ever have. They are painfully aware of their own confusion. In large numbers, they have lost faith in traditional religion (they see it as divisive), but at the same time they no longer seek salvation in either science or other myths of human progress. They are generally suspicious of institutions, and they resist creeds, categories and coercion. As a general rule they are less likely to think in dualistic and polarizing ways that divide the world into black and white, Left and Right or conservative and liberal. Nor are they inclined to see others in exclusionary ways or appreciate those who do. At the same time they more readily acknowledge their own lostness, and they spiritually hunger for something else, something better than they have known. With enough focus, thought, courage, love and sacrifice, we can become that something better.

Could we imagine a Christian grassroots movement where every individual—regardless of race, gender or class—matters and has a voice? Could we imagine a community of faith that is light on outdated creed, tradition and dogma, but heavy on free inquiry, honest discussion and empathy for the viewpoints of others? Could we imagine a church light on hierarchy but heavy on open, caring relationships? Could we imagine local gatherings of Christians who don't look to

Rome or Canterbury or Washington for direction? Instead, truths are discovered in the finest way possible, by being personally drawn from study of scripture, then discussed in groups, and finally tested and lived out in active loving service in our neighborhoods. Could we imagine spiritual centers that empower people to study and think for themselves, to make moral decisions, and be reborn and reformed into the image of Christ, becoming thereby genuinely new and more loving people than they otherwise would be?

Can we picture gatherings where Jesus is taught as the way of grace, trust, forgiveness, service and love? Can we picture a worldwide network of communities devoted to a ministry of reconciliation, seeking to heal our planet's otherwise angry, bitter, partisan divisions? Can we picture settings where sin and failure and shame can be freely, openly confessed to one another so that no one in such loving community need ever again be alone at night in a losing battle? Can we picture a place where all genuine believers, indeed all genuine seekers, are fully welcomed to live, serve, learn and express their faith together? Can we picture a church that celebrates faith in Christ in all its colorful cultural diversity while joyfully and confidently offering to everyone a chance to start over—a transcendent experience of spiritual rebirth and resurrection? Can we see it? Can we be it? If so, our children and our children's children will be with us, and we will be the church of tomorrow while remaining true to the church at first.

The path to the place to which God calls us is illuminated still by restorationist longings. Throughout the centuries-long story of faith, the church has been served well again and again by those who sought restoration, whether their objective was the *imago dei* (the re-formation within us of the image of God, a common monastic quest) or the *vita apostolica* (the apostolic life, the goal of Franciscans and others) or the *ecclesia primitiva* (the primitive church, the vision which in-spired many medieval reform and dissident movements as well as sixteenth-century European and nineteenth-century American restoration movements). Many such movements contributed richly to the ongoing story and continued to make important contributions until later generations buried the original spiritual light beneath layers of ritual, law and dogma.

A Final Farewell to the Twelfth Century

Scripture, History and Vision

Again and again we return to a close reading of scripture. Yes, scripture is unique, reliable and normative, but it needs always to be accepted on its own terms. We cannot claim for it what it does not claim for itself; certainly we cannot claim for it what it specifically denies for itself. We cannot flat-line into law—in direct violation of new covenant teaching (Rom. 6:14; 7:6; 10:4; 2 Cor. 3:3-6; the whole point of Galatians)—all its epics of world origins, its sparkling historical narratives, its works of penetrating philosophical reflection, its prayers and songs, its prophetic oracles in all their passionate moral splendor, its manuals for discipleship drawn from the life and teachings of Jesus, its letters to young churches leading them to real-life solutions to real-life problems, and its stunning apocalyptic visions.

As we read scripture, we will thrill to the exodus of the slave nation Israel as it escapes oppression. We will be challenged by the burning moral passion of the prophets. We will be astonished by the raw emotional honesty of the psalms and letters. We will be deeply moved and then transformed as we contemplate the cross and resurrection of Jesus and begin to see what it really means. Eventually we will sense that through these pages God is calling us into a living, trusting and loving relationship with him. He is confronting us with what is mysterious and transcendent and sacred in life and inviting us into that realm of awe and wonder where personal growth best happens. Scripture forces us to ponder the complexities of life. It reveals human nature as it is—complicated, elusive and unpredictable—but then shows us a way to live appreciatively and productively in a world such as ours with all its marvelous diversity and grandeur. And gradually we begin to understand and experience the real story of which our life stories have always been a part.

One caution, in particular, is in order. In our efforts to recover the faith, life and spirit of the church at first, it is important that we take care to distinguish between what the New Testament says about the new life in Christ and the degree of implementation possible in the first century. It was failure to do this that led many churches in the years leading up to the Civil War to claim a biblical mandate for slavery.

Likewise, in our time the restrictions on women in 1 Corinthians 14 and 1 Timothy 2 have to be understood in their literary and historical contexts, as all scripture does. In fact, interpreting any document of any kind depends on understanding its historical context and original intent. This is the cardinal rule of interpretation, and interpreters always do this except when for some reason—usually cultural—they don't want to; it is for this reason that we do not wash one another's feet, greet one another with holy kisses or insist on women wearing veils during worship.

Once grasped, the truth that all texts are best understood in their historical contexts makes instantaneous sense. It's like a light bulb going on, and it immediately restores consistency to both our interpretation and application of scripture. Paul was asking Christian women in the first-century cities of Corinth and Ephesus to accommodate to contemporary standards of decency which in that time meant absolute submission to the life-and-death authority of the *paterfamilias*. He was guiding Christians in the setting in which they lived; he was not making their setting valid and mandatory for all time.[6] God was no more making a case for eternally silencing women in worship than for keeping slavery forever slavery. It really is that simple: If God wants women silent in the churches forever, he also wants submissive slaves forever (Eph. 6:5-9; Col. 3:22-4:1; Titus 2:9-10; 1 Pet. 2:18-25). And churches that continue to insist on women's silence in church are even now in the same process of losing moral credibility as pro-slavery churches did in the shadow and aftermath of the Civil War, their ethical and evangelistic witness crippled by resisting a principle of justice that one day all will see.

If, however, we listen to Jesus, we have every reason for confidence. He tells us that we must no longer, if we would be his followers, think in terms of domination and subordination, of who is greatest, of who exercises authority over whom. He tells us that the one who would be great must be the servant. He tells us that the power in life is in self-sacrificial love, in empowering others, in giving up our power so that all may become empowered, and this he unforgettably demonstrated by his own death.

A Final Farewell to the Twelfth Century

If we understand what he is saying and act accordingly, one day patterns of abuse and discrimination will end. It's all part of God's will being done on earth as it is in heaven. One day all people everywhere will be judged not by the categories of their physical birth—as they were in the Neoplatonic world that is passing away—but by the maturity of their spiritual rebirth. One day those who are in Christ's church will again be the most ethical, humane and lovingly involved people on earth, and their witness will be seen by all. We will live radiant, transformed lives freed from sin, fear, lust and prejudice—freed, in fact, from all that holds us back as children of God. Then our light will break forth like the dawn, a light that promises to all men and women everywhere that whoever they are and whatever they have done they can start over, be reborn, be forgiven, and then discover within themselves the Spirit of God.

Now to be truly Christ's church on earth we bid at long last a final farewell to the twelfth century. The age of castles, fortresses and high walls is over. Its theology of fear and dark enchantment has lost its hold on our imaginations. We will not again subject ourselves to dynasties of lawyer popes, to those who would impose on us purely legal understandings of Jesus, church and gospel. Gospel will be resurrected as the controlling metaphor by which we structure and experience faith and life and community. No longer will anyone be driven to the sidelines of the church simply because they were born one way or another. We will leave the twelfth century with its Neoplatonic fascination with category and hierarchy far behind and enter courageously with Jesus into the twenty-first.

Notes

1. R. W. Southern, *Western Society and the Church in the Middle Ages* (New York: Viking Penguin, 1970, 1985), 37.

2. Previously aristocratic women had exercised considerable power, influence and control in the church as queens, landowners and even some-

times abbesses of monasteries that included both men and women. However, when the increasing militarized church of Gregory VII and his successors resorted to inflammatory anti-female attacks in their insistence on the celibacy of the clergy and when furthermore their aggressive pursuit of property rights led, in aristocratic response, to primogeniture (inheritance by the oldest son) as the dominant inheritance pattern, women were doubly marginalized. To begin to understand this sordid chapter in church history, see: Suzanne Fonay Wemple, *Women in Frankish Society: Marriage and the Cloister, 500-900* (Philadelphia: University of Pennsylvania, 1981); Jo Ann McNamara and Suzanne Wemple, "The Power of Women through the Family in Medieval Europe: 500-1100," *Feminist Studies* 1 (Winter-Spring 1973); C. N. L. Brooke, "Gregorian Reform in Action: Clerical Marriage in England, 1050-1200," (1956), *Change in Medieval Society* (ed. Sylvia L. Thrupp; New York: Appleton-Century-Crofts, 1964): 49-71; Anne Llewellyn Barstow, *Married Priests and the Reforming Papacy: The Eleventh-Century Debates* (New York: Edwin Mellen, 1982).

3. Harold J. Berman, *Law and Revolution: The Formation of the Western Legal Tradition* (Cambridge, MA: Harvard University, 1983), 38.

4. I'm indebted for these observations to Leon J. Podles, *The Church Impotent: The Feminization of Christianity* (Dallas: Spence, 1999).

5. Richard T. Hughes and C. Leonard Allen, *Illusions of Innocence: Protestant Primitivism in America, 1630-1875* (Chicago: University of Chicago, 1988), 1-24.

6. Craig S. Keener, *Paul, Women & Wives: Marriage and Women's Ministry in the Letters of Paul* (Peabody, MA: Hendrickson, 1992), 185.

9

Tradition: The Rural Church's Vehicle for Change

Rodger Weems

Robert Fulghum opens one of his books with a story about a small-town fire department summoned to a house where smoke was pouring from an upstairs window. The crew broke in and found a man in a smoldering bed. After the man was rescued and the mattress doused, the obvious question was asked: "How did it happen?"

"I don't know," the man replied. "It was on fire when I lay down on it."[1]

That, says Fulghum, is the human condition, a lifestory in a sentence: "out of the frying pan, and into the hot water." We mindlessly repeat habits, even after changing circumstances make those behaviors irrelevant or even self-destructive. We spend our lives lying down on burning beds, wondering why the same actions that once brought rest and comfort now hurt so badly.

Nowhere is the tension over change more painful than in small town America. The pain may be less obvious than in urban America, but it is no less real. Peel back the stiff-lipped stoicism and civic pride, and you will find small towns all over America desperately worried about their futures.

Churches share those worries. Church members, rural or urban, are not immune to the upheavals of social change. In Churches of Christ in the United States, most of our members now reside in cities or suburbs. But the majority of our congregations are still in rural areas. To some degree, the health of the church can be measured by the health of its small towns. Sadly, many of our small-town churches are not very healthy, struggling to fight off decline and death. For many rural churches, the words of the hymn are taken literally: "Change and decay in all around I see."

More than any other segment of American life, small towns are tradition-based societies. Order and predictability are the governing principles. Change can and does occur, but at a far different pace than in the city. This poses some particular challenges for the small-town church trying to cope with a rapidly changing world.

Are rural churches doomed to repeat their habits until they die? Must they continue lying down on burning beds until they suffocate or are consumed? Some evidence suggests a bleak future for the small-town church, but there is a different approach: use tradition as a springboard for wholesome change. Marry the past to the future. Use tradition as a foundation for growth and improvement, not a shackle that binds.

I know the concept sounds preposterous, but Christianity is full of paradoxes. Remember that our faith was founded by a dead man who came back to life. Do we dare dismiss anything as impossible?

The Need for a Cultural Anthropology of Rural America

Before a missionary takes up residence in a foreign field, he will want to do a "cultural anthropology" of his chosen field. (Cultural anthropology is the study of groups of people in their environments.) The study may be formal or informal, but the missionary will try to learn something about the language, history, economy and geography of the place where he hopes to preach the gospel. If he is wise, he will find out all he can about the motives, attitudes, ambitions, fears and loves of the people he seeks to reach. What are their strengths? What are their problems? What are their temptations?

This time-consuming step may frustrate the prospective missionary, who is anxious to plunge into the serious business of winning people to Christ. But it will save him a world of frustration and failure later. No matter how capable the missionary may be, he will be ineffective if he carries with him assumptions from his own background and expects them always to hold true in the new situation. Few things are more heartbreaking than trying to preach Christ to people you love, but with whom you cannot connect, because they are so different from yourself. The wise missionary will not expect the culture to adapt to him. He must adapt to the culture, without selling out his faith and integrity.

It is just as important to study the culture at home as it is in the mission field. Because we usually speak a common language and share some part of a common heritage, it might be assumed that cultural studies are not needed in the United States, but that assumption is flawed.

Once, American church life was based on a rural model. When the United States was an agricultural nation, churches developed strategies, programs and styles that suited rural life. Sunday services were scheduled at 11:00 a.m., allowing worshippers to tend to animals and do chores before worshipping. Summer gospel meetings were held in the idle time when crops were "laid by," after planting but before harvest, when families were not needed in the fields and had time for extended periods of worship, study and fellowship. Programs and activities, styles of leadership, and a whole host of other factors were borrowed from rural life and transported to the cities without much thought.

America became a nation of urbanites, but the church retained many of its rural traditions long after they failed to work in cities, where the rhythms of work and leisure were different. Many urban congregations, once filled by rural transplants, disappeared or became ineffective when the generation that founded them died.

Church growth literature of recent years has done an effective job of de-mystifying American culture, which is vastly different from the culture of the past. The gospel message is unchanging: "the same yesterday, today, and forever." But beyond question, the strategies and techniques that were once effective in leading rural people to faith do not work well in cities.

Authors like Rick Warren have been especially helpful for believers in Christ as they come to grips with a changing culture. Warren helped build Saddleback Community Church (a Baptist church that prefers not to be called "Baptist") into a huge megachurch in Southern California. Warren's book *The Purpose-Driven Church* encourages each local church to understand its "target" for evangelism—the person who lives in its community.[2]

Warren's message is a sound one: understand what motivates your target and develop a strategy to reach him, without compromising your message and mission. Unfortunately, despite repeated warnings from Warren not to adopt Saddleback Community Church's strategies wholesale, that is exactly what many churches, urban and rural, have done.

For rural churches this mistake can be especially damaging. Just as some urban churches held on too long to rural strategies long after they became ineffective, many rural churches are copying urban methods in a desperate attempt to stay alive.

Bradley Creed is a professor at Baylor University's George W. Truett Seminary and an expert on the application of rural sociology to the small-town church. Dr. Creed has said, "The most dangerous month in the life of a small-town Baptist preacher is the month after the Convention. He hears all kinds of wonderful church growth ideas, takes them home, applies them inappropriately, and gets himself fired." Firing the preacher is the least of the damage.

Baptist churches are not the only churches that have suffered because of inappropriate application of urban church growth ideas to rural church life, where they often lead to conflict and decline, not to the growth and life that was intended.

To help his members understand their target for evangelism, Rick Warren created a caricature of the kind of person Saddleback Community Church was trying to reach. He named him Saddleback Sam. Saddleback Sam is an urban professional, the kind of person who lives near the church where Warren preaches. To interest him with the gospel a church must employ strategies that appeal to him, without compromising the integrity of the gospel message. But borrowing a set of methods designed to win Saddleback Sam to Christ, and expecting those methods to work in small towns without substantial adaptation, makes no more sense than lying down on a burning bed, on the reasoning that one has always gone to bed at the same time.

To understand the differences between urban and rural people, I developed a caricature of the evangelistic target in the community where I lived: Stephenville, Texas, a town of about 16,000 people 70 miles west of Fort Worth. It is a community that describes itself as "The Cowboy Capital of the World." An area whose economy is based on the dairy industry, it is the top milk-producing county in Texas. The city square contains a "Rodeo Walk of Fame"; bronze plaques bearing the names of famous rodeo cowboys and cowgirls, many of them from Stephenville, are set into the sidewalk.

Like his urban counterpart, "Stephenville Sam" is a caricature. Caricatures are generalizations, if not exaggerations. They oversimplify, describing the prevailing culture but are inadequate to describe every person's complexity. Still, they can be helpful.

Each church should custom tailor its own picture. In the urban church, Seattle Sam is different from Saddleback Sam; San Antonio Sam might have Hispanic features. The rural church should also be sensitive to its setting. In the south Texas fishing village, Seadrift Sam might be a Vietnamese fisherman, requiring vastly different strategies than those designed to reach the central Texas cowboy.

The point cannot be repeated too many times: please don't borrow somebody else's picture or copy some other church's programs without first localizing them. You will fail if you do. Paint your own picture of your church's target for evangelism, and develop your own strategy.

Understanding the Rural Mindset

Gary Farley is director of the Center for Rural Church Leadership in Carrolton, Alabama. He has developed a list of qualities that distinguish rural churches from urban ones. The list, which deals primarily with cultural differences, is presented below, with some minor adaptations for Churches of Christ:

Contrasting Church Cultures

Large/Suburban	*Small/Rural*
2 or 3 generations or less	4 or 5 generations
Boomer led	Builder led
Leaders remember Vietnam and Watergate	Leaders remember Depression and World War II
Upwardly mobile members	Stable Socio-economic status for members
Church in debt	Debt-free
Evangelistic focus is central	Service to members is actual focus
Hire help	Do it yourself
Probable life cycle 50 years	Century or more and still sticking
Narrow band of social class	Broad band of social class
Significant turnover of members	Many with ancestors in graveyard
Diversity of occupations	Narrow band of vocations
Delegate	Hands-on
Creating its story and culture	Living out its history and culture
Members relate selectively to church	Broad involvement of members in programs
Limited bonds in the congregation	Members are bonded in several ways—family, friends, business
See others mostly at church	See others in day by day walk
Conflict as a process	Conflict avoided at all cost
Want to be led to the Promised Land	Want to get back to Eden
Worship as praise	Worship as proclamation
Did it help me?	Was my family there?
Focus on the event	Focus on relational elements
Dress for comfort at worship	May dress more formally at worship
Draw on wide resources	Loyal to brotherhood resources & programs
Cosmopolitan perspective	Local perspective
Drive SUV's	Drive real pickup trucks
Contemporary Christian music	Locally relevant music (eg Southern Gospel)
Minister much like the members	Minister much like the members[3]

Debunking Myths about Rural America

The differences between urban and rural life in American are real and far-reaching. However, there are some myths about rural American life that need to be debunked, as they sometimes prevent rural and urban Christians from understanding and relating to each other.

(1) *Rural people don't work as hard.* The different rhythms of work and leisure in cities and small towns may fool urbanites into believing that rural life is relaxed and slow-paced. Because small towns thrive on relationships and spend a great deal of time cultivating them, they may falsely leave the impression that rural people do not work very hard. A lack of traffic congestion and lack of a commute, which produce a lower stress level, may leave the impression that rural people put in fewer hours on the job. The impression is also fueled by the long-standing rural social convention of making "small talk" before entering into important business transactions, suggesting a relaxed atmosphere.

The rural worker works just as many hours as his urban counterpart, though they may not be the same hours. As proof of that fact, one need only count the number of farms during harvest season in which farm equipment operates by headlights, well after dark. Further, the same waitress who serves the farmer breakfast in the small town cafe may very well serve his evening meal.

(2) *Small-town people are anti-technology.* Rural people are no more or less likely to embrace technology than their big-city counterparts. Satellite television's first customers were rural residents, who were too scattered to make cable TV economical. Now, telecommuting is bringing to the country a new wave of residents, who live where they choose rather than where their jobs demand.

The June 2000 issue of *Soybean Digest*—a rural journal if ever there were one—was a special issue on "Farming the Internet." One article tells of a Plainview, Texas cotton farmer who saves $50,000 per year by ordering farm chemicals via the Internet. But the same article emphasizes that farmers are just as reliant on service from local farm equipment dealers as ever.[4]

Churches could take a lesson from agri-business, which has has swiftly adapted to changing technology, while retaining the "local flavor" so important to success in small town life.

My Own Story

For me, this study is not just academic; I struggled for years to find a way to be effective in the 120-year-old church to which the Lord had called me. My first few years in Stephenville were characterized by frustration. I was angry because I thought the church had lied to me. In my interviews with the congregation before the position of minister was offered to me, I was told of the wonderful things the church wished to do, the improvements the church wished to make, and the plans for the future that were being formulated.

But when I moved to Stephenville and attempted to implement the very things the church had spoken of in the interview, the answer was always, "No; not yet; not now; not that way." I did not have the maturity to realize that the desire for change and the downward pull of outmoded methods and traditions could coexist in the same church. This way of doing things was not healthy, but it was not dishonest.

It took me about three years to realize that the church had not misrepresented its intentions to me; I had merely underestimated the downward tug of the burning bed. The church genuinely believed it could grow again while continuing to do the very things that had led it into decline. Traditions—even destructive ones—die hard, and denial of reality dies even harder.

At times, it seems that small-town churches are doomed for a collision between long-time residents and newcomers, between older and younger generations. This is particularly true of rural communities in transition, where small-town population is swelled by migration from cities. But small-town churches can change for the better in healthy, wholesome, loving ways. War is not inevitable. This plan calls for honoring the past, while planning decisively for the future.

Small-town churches operate out of their history. Their traditions are their most cherished possessions. Their focus is not on tomorrow but on yesterday; there is no stronger motivation for the church's long-term members than to preserve their heritage and history. Try as I may, I could not change that fact. I would more likely succeed at repealing the law of gravity than at changing that characteristic of rural life.

My spiritual and emotional struggle to be effective in a church that truly wanted to improve but was mired in the past led me to three guiding principles to lead the church toward positive change:

(1) *I cannot change others, so I must change myself.* This axiom from psychotherapy is trite but often ignored, especially in church life. I could not force change on the congregation, even when a majority agreed it was desperately needed. I had to change my own attitudes and methods. This opened the gateway for the church and its leaders to change theirs.

I began honoring our congregation's past, listening to its stories, developing an interest in its history, some of which was remarkable. For example, I learned that every adult male in Stephenville participated, with either money or labor, in constructing the church's original 1888 building. I learned that our congregation had Stephenville's only full-time minister during World War II, and that a major part of his duties consisted of performing dozens of weddings for military personnel and their brides, who were of many faiths. Both stories are worth retelling.

Not all tradition is bitter and destructive; some is comforting and inspiring. As I loosened my grip, allowing long-term members to own their past, they loosened their own grasps, allowing younger members to own their future. It hasn't worked perfectly, but it has been a good trade-off.

Of course, there is always a danger that a leader who changes his attitude will merely "sell out," will become mired in unhealthy traditions himself, and will become part of the problem rather than part of the solution. But it doesn't have to be that way. I have asked my friends to keep an eye on me, and to inform me when I am misreading the climate of the church. Sometimes, the church is ready for an improvement I don't perceive.

(2) *You cannot "move on" from loss until you have first grieved it.* This is another principle from psychotherapy. Life's losses—whether

a spouse, a job, a child or a congregation that can never return to the past—must be grieved. The widow understands that life must go on after her husband dies, but she will resent anyone whom she perceives to take away her husband's memory. She will also resent being pushed to "get over it" while she is still grieving.

For long-time church members, the loss of the "good old days," in which church life was sweet and simple, is very real. No matter how needed change was, it was insensitive of me to push for it without first giving our people an opportunity to grieve a past that could never be recaptured. Consequently, we began including some element of our congregation's history in every important change the church made. When we dedicated the church's new family center (which contained Stephenville's only church gymnasium) we asked our members to loan photographs of past church events. Some of these photographs were enlarged and included in an attractive display, which was featured during the dedication ceremony.

(3) *Change must be sponsored*. This suggestion comes from professional fundraisers. The most important factor in whether a prospective donor gives is who does the asking. An appeal for a marginal cause, made by a person whom the donor knows and trusts, will raise more money than a worthier cause for which a stranger makes the appeal.

In the local church—especially the small-town church—change must be sponsored or it will not occur. New people must also be "sponsored" before their ideas are taken seriously. This fact is unpleasant and reveals one of the darker sides of rural church life, but I am convinced it is true.

There is no finer service a long-term member of a church struggling to grow can make to the kingdom of God than to "sponsor" new people. This means taking the new member under his wing, introducing him and praising him to other long-term members, thereby "loaning" to the newcomer his own credibility, until the newcomer can be accepted on his own merit. "Sponsoring" a new member shortens the length of time before his ideas are taken seriously.

For the minister of a small-town church, this means his efforts to bring about positive change will not likely be taken seriously for several years. This is a bitter pill to swallow—it certainly was for me—but short of terrible infighting and division, there usually is no other way. The small-town preacher should count on taking years before he earns enough credibility and respect to be able to lead the church through change. And he must accept the truth—bitter or not—that for several years he will be a "hired hand," not a valued partner in the important decisions of the congregation.

This is consistent with George Barna's analysis in his 1993 book, *Turn-Around Churches*. Barna estimated that bringing systemic change to a traditional church usually requires a minimum of four year.[5] In my experience, a rural church most likely requires a decade.

During those years, he builds credibility with the people by lovingly serving them: burying their dead, marrying their children, visiting them when they are sick, and crying with them when they are in trouble. Over time, the people will decide that he is believable and will hear—even welcome—his suggestions for improving the church.

I know that this slow, patient method of bringing about change runs against the grain of popular culture, in which change occurs at lightning speed. But for the established church, steeped in tradition, there is no other way, short of a bitter church split.

More importantly, this method is deeply biblical. In Isaiah 65:2, the Lord said, "All day long I have held out my hands to an obstinate people." What behavior better describes obstinance than preferring destructive, but familiar, behaviors to positive change? In my case change in the church began coming more easily when I stopped offering the people a clenched fist and began offering them an open hand.

If such advice seems hard to accept, consider this: traditionalists are not the only ones drawn by the destructive, downward pull of the burning bed. Agents of change may continue in ineffective ways too.

Recently I spoke with a highly capable young minister who preaches for a small-town church that has experienced a great migration of urbanites. Of course, the church is struggling with issues of change and identity. Like this young minister, each of his two predecessors was skilled, articulate and dedicated. Each minister pushed the church for change at a faster pace than it was ready to accept, and each minister was dismissed, having accomplished only a fraction of what he had intended. My young friend is also frustrated because the church will not change at the pace he believes it should. He is pushing hard and is meeting the same resistance his two predecessors did. In his eyes I saw a younger reflection of myself.

The patient approach has little appeal for this dynamic young preacher. However, in view of the failure of his predecessors, perhaps a question is in order: who is holding on to ineffective methods, the "traditionalist" or the "change agent." Whose bed is on fire?

Notes

1. Robert Fulghum, *It Was on Fire When I Lay Down on It* (New York: Ivy Books, 1988).

2. Rick Warren, *The Purpose Driven Church* (Grand Rapids, MI: Zondervan, 1995).

3. Gary Farley, www. ruralchurch.org

4. John Russnogle and Fae Holin, "Farmer Feedback," *Soybean Journal* (June 2000), 28-30.

5. George Barna, *Turn-Around Churches* (Ventura, CA: Regal, 1993), 56-57.

10

Mission Impossible?

Chris Smith

What does the future hold for Churches of Christ? Where will we be as an institution 20 years from now? Sometimes on a blue Monday following a bad Sunday, I wonder if I will be the last one my age left in Churches of Christ a generation from now. While we are an established group of over a million strong and no longer reside on the other side of the tracks, there are ominous clouds of concern on the horizon.

Growth Rate

Recently I attended a minister's luncheon that was attended by representatives of the three major branches of the Restoration Movement. While the fellowship was enjoyable, the repeated refrain was disconcerting: "I pastor New Salem Christian Church (Disciples of Christ). We are 50 years old. Our heyday was 25 years ago. We are trying to rebuild." What no one said was the complete and brutal truth: "My church is one generation from death and my mission is one of maintenance only." The message of decline is a familiar one among mainline Protestant denominations. After enjoying good growth in the first half of the twentieth century, the last few decades have not been as kind, with some groups experiencing drops of 20% in membership.[1]

When we look at Churches of Christ the picture is not as bleak, but the colors are the same. We are not growing. According to Mac Lynn in the 2000 edition of *Churches of Christ in the United States*, the total number of congregations and membership in the United States has declined slightly since 1990, and these numbers are not significantly higher than 1980.[2] We have not kept up with the population growth, especially in new people groups and minorities. Over the last 20 years our growth has been nominal at best. The curve of decline may be 20 years behind other religious groups, but the trend is there nevertheless.

The Generational Thing

Much has been written on the topic of generations since Strauss and Howe published their book, *Generations,* in 1991.[3] Many have chronicled the impact of the Baby Boom generation (born 1943-1960). This huge group has been compared to the pig moving through the python of society and culture. Fifteen years ago academics and theologians wondered what impact boomers would have on churches as they returned to organized religion after their college years. Now economists try to predict the affect of boomers on the Social Security system and retirement funds.

Within Churches of Christ Baby Boomers have been moving into leadership roles over the last ten years. With this move into leadership changes have come, along with increased conflict and strife. For example, congregations—especially large urban and suburban ones—that have not experienced tension over worship style are rare. Boomers, who because of their sheer size are accustomed to having their way, are expressing a desire for less rigidity in worship, greater freedom of expression, small-group community and less attention to tradition. The greatest generational conflict has taken place between boomers and the G.I. generation (born 1901-1924). The War generation established or built up most of the churches that these boomers now desire to change.

Boomers, who will comprise the leadership group for at least another 15 years, have two characteristics that do not bode well for churches: high expectations along with low institutional loyalty. Boomers

Mission Impossible?

expect the best and even believe they deserve the best, whether it is a vehicle purchase, medical care, school system or church. If you doubt this trait, ask any of our youth workers about parental expectations of their ministries. Coupled with this is the fact that boomers commit slowly to organized groups and will bolt when things do not go their way. Boomers join groups because of felt needs, not loyalty or duty or for the overall good of society. A boomer mother will join the PTA, not because she is supposed to, but because she thinks it will help her fourth grader.

Sometimes the smallest of changes can alert one to an overall cultural shift. Within the past ten years I have observed how long people will visit a congregation before "placing membership." What people used to do in a month or less, now takes up to a year. Some never place membership, but choose to keep their options open and visit from church to church. It is not uncommon to find as many as 20% of people in a given church who are floaters—people who never commit.

This lack of institutional loyalty also translates into another trait. If boomers do not get their way, they leave. They will not stay around and argue forever. They seem to have little tolerance for a fight. More church splits or divisions seem to be taking place now as more boomers move into leadership roles, but far more often boomers just leave, quietly but steadily. They leave for a more progressive or conservative Church of Christ, the community church down the street, the church with the great children's ministry—whatever church fulfills their felt needs. It is increasingly rare to find a church member in my hometown of Nashville, Tennessee, who has attended the same congregation for over twenty years. Most churches experience a revolving door of people coming and going, looking for a church that better suits them.[4] An added phenomenon is the number of parents who attend one congregation while allowing their teenage children to worship elsewhere. The idea of a family worshiping together has given way to having needs met.

Finally it is becoming obvious that tension exists between the Boomers and Generation X (born 1961-1981). To the amazement of the Boomer, Generation X and the Millennial Generation (born after

1981) do not necessarily want to worship the same way as Boomers. For example, I was surprised at our recent summer camp to see the Gen X leaders take over two hours to baptize four children. Frequent prayers, testimonials, the singing of repetitive songs—it seemed as if they could have gone on all night. Tears flowed and emotions reigned. I kept looking for Bible study and wondered why they could not have kept it to an hour.

Generation X is even less committed to institutions than Boomers, and they struggle with the idea of absolutes. While churched Gen Xers may not be "as bad" when it comes to disbelief in absolutes, for them the ultimate sin is to be judgmental and denominational distinctions mean almost nothing. Commitment to radical discipleship, however, is another matter. It may be that this generation will provide more missionaries to third-world countries than their more self-centered older brother.

Three Solutions

Church growth is an inexact science. Perhaps in no other field is it more true that "Statistics don't lie but statisticians do." Determining what makes a church grow in a given locale ought to be easy, but it is not. Sometimes when our congregations grow we can point to specific actions taken and be reasonably sure of our conclusions. Other times we just do not know what led to the growth, or we do not know why what seemed to work in the past does not work anymore. We scurry around in an attempt to catch the latest wave. Probably every church leader has had the experience of going to the pastor's conference or lectureship and learning of the new "can't miss" program. Coming home in the flush of excitement, the program is implemented and twelve months later the post mortem is read. Some of our congregations, for example, are now learning of the difficulty of implementing Saddleback's purpose-driven model in an existing church. Their simple baseball approach to ministry, moving people from one level of commitment to another, often results not in growth but balks and passed balls. Not withstanding these caveats, I offer the following three suggestions for church growth. The first two are given in the spirit of "maybe it will work, maybe it won't." We have known all along that the third solution is right, whether we have wanted to admit it or not.

1. Reinvention

Churches of Christ have long proclaimed, with varying degrees of success, that we wanted to be Christians only while not claiming to be the only Christians. This plea has been largely lost in our move toward denominationalism over the last century. We no longer call people to be just Christians, nor do our people think of themselves as Christians only. Except for national headquarters, we have all the trappings of other Christian groups. There are Church of Christ schools, preachers and lectureships. Sunday school material, which has been carefully screened for doctrinal correctness, can be purchased from competing bookstores. While we use euphemistic terms to describe ourselves, like "our fellowship," "the brotherhood," or "the church," to no one's surprise but ourselves we have become a denomination. We are Church of Christ.

But it seems we have become an established religious group at exactly the wrong time. Denominations apparently are no longer in favor. The fastest growing religious groups in the United States, according to Flavil Yeakley, are independent charismatic churches and independent non-charismatic churches. Independent community churches, which shy away from denominational affiliation, are booming. The two most well known are Saddleback Community Church in Orange County, California and the Willow Creek Church in a suburb of Chi-cago. Yet almost any city of any size now boasts a community church that is bordering on becoming a megachurch. In a recent conversation with a minister of a Nashville community church, I learned of their phenomenal growth from 200 to 3000 in eight years. While they are siphoning members from other churches with an energetic worship service and a felt-need approach to ministry, they are also reaching their target audience of the unchurched. Last year they baptized over 150, the majority of whom would have had little church background.

While doctrinal stances vary from one community church to another, their rhetoric is clearly non-denominational. They apparently just want to be Christians. They have stolen our forsaken message and are now singing our song. In addition to the non-denominational status of the community churches, other traits include contemporary worship and small groups. The organ has been replaced with a band, and the Sunday school has been transformed into a Thursday night cell group. The above-mentioned community church recently completed a multi-million-dollar building program. They were not overly concerned with the fact that they ran out of money and could not presently build adult Bible school classrooms. Adults meet throughout the week in a variety of small groups. On the weekend they bring thousands together for worship, meeting on Saturday and Sunday in a theatre style auditorium equipped with the latest in lighting and sound.

Some in our fellowship have moved in the direction of the community church model, opting to drop the name "Church of Christ" or to de-emphasize it, much like Saddleback disguises its affiliation with the Southern Baptist Convention. These churches claim the name "Church of Christ" carries with it so much negative baggage that an alternative name must be used. Some of these groups remain a cappella while others believe that instrumental music must be a part of worship to reach those on the outside. The target audience of such churches, while perhaps not as blatantly one-dimensional as Willow Creek, is the baby boomer. The attempt is to enclose the wine of the gospel in a new wineskin that is more appealing to those under fifty. (In coming years more congregations will be started by Gen Xers that will appeal to their generation.) Less emphasis is placed on traditional issues important to Churches of Christ in the past, like instrumental music or doctrinal differences with other conservative Christian groups. More emphasis is placed on relationships, both with God and with each other. One successful community church has as their cherished slogan; "We just love people where they are."[5]

Others have maintained closer ties with our fellowship and kept the name on the sign, yet are trying to break out of a traditional mode as well. Newer songs, praise teams, extensive use of technology, drama presentations, small groups—all these "innovations" are being promoted as a way to connect with the current culture. Behind many of the changes is the unspoken sentiment that if the boomers become more proud of their local church, they will become more evangelistic or energetic. Those promoting reinvention claim that boomers really do want to be committed. The commitment, however, is to God and Jesus and not the form that has characterized Churches of Christ in the past.

2. Plant Churches

Numerous studies have shown that the most effective way to evangelize is to start new churches. The correlation between total membership and number of churches has been proven over and again. If a denominational group wants more adherents in a particular area, all they have to do is start more churches.[6]

New churches are needed to reach new community growth. Scores of churches were started in new suburbs all across the country in the 1950s. It is no coincidence that most religious groups experienced significant growth in the 50s as well. Wherever there is new community growth, a congregation should be planted. People new to a community and unchurched people as well are far more likely to attend a new congregation rather than an older one.

New churches are effective in reaching new cultural groups. If the neighborhood changes from white to African-American, no matter how hard the existing church may try, it will not be as effective in reaching the newcomers as a newly established African-American congregation. If the neighborhood is changing or immigrants are moving in, wonderful opportunities exist for new churches. Several metropolitan areas are seeing new congregations spring up in the inner city as established congregations move further out into the suburbs. Congregational "white flight" would not produce such a stigma of guilt if these churches went out of their way to establish new congregations in the areas of town they were leaving.

Planting churches forces groups to maintain priorities. One community church planter in the Dallas area has started six congregations in ten years.[7] Recently his congregation sent off forty families to start another body, leaving the mother church with less than 200 members—again. An outside observer noted, "I'll say this, it sure forces them to be evangelistic." This church, which still meets in rented facilities and has had its share of ups and downs, can today claim over 1000 children, grandchildren and even great grandchildren. This "mother church" model was seen many times in the 50s and 60s. Churches like the Coleman Avenue congregation in Memphis started several daughter churches by sending out groups of members. Today, unfortunately, it seems we can only think of building large congregations, doing our best to keep everybody close to home.

Starting new congregations also provides leadership opportunities for new generations. Instead of the constant tension between generations, boomers and busters alike can organize churches that appeal to their peers. Good leaders intuitively know what "connects" with their generation. They should take these intuitions and move ahead. Convincing others in a local church that change must take place can be taxing and time consuming, wasting efforts that could be spent reaching those on the outside. The danger, of course, is that we will all eventually reside in single generation churches, having little appreciation for each other.

New churches grow faster and have a higher baptism ratio than older churches. There seems to be no escaping the fact that few churches experience growth after 25 years of existence. My own experience in ministry illustrates this growth pattern. I have been blessed to work with four fine congregations in four different cities over the last 20 years. The first three churches were started in 1949, 1953, 1960, and the fourth, although much older, became new by relocating in the late 60s. All are situated in the suburbs and have good leadership. The churches have vibrant programs of work, have been heavy supporters of missions and built facilities that were more than adequate. My family and I have been blessed and loved by all four churches. But the cold hard facts are these: none of the four is currently growing and all are smaller in attendance than their previous high. The 1949 church stopped growing 13 years ago, the 1953 church stopped 22 years ago, the 1960 church stopped nine years ago and the relocated church four years ago.[8] These churches have followed the almost inevitable life cycle of churches: years of growth followed by a period of plateau. And only 5% of these plateaued churches ever grow again.

One aspect of the community church phenomenon that is sometimes overlooked is that these churches are new church plants. I suggest that the key to growth may not be so much that community churches have tapped into the current sociological bias against denominations; the key may be simply that independents are starting more churches than old-line denominations. The question for us as a fellowship is this: what would the impact on our growth rate be if every healthy church over 200 members started another congregation in the next five years?

3. Recover a Sense of Evangelism

Evangelism in mainstream Churches of Christ has been out of favor for 25 years. My earliest memories as a young preacher in the late 70s are of a fellowship determined to fight the "Crossroads" movement. Extensive energy was expended on pointing out the failures of this movement—its legalism, divisiveness and so forth. But an unexpected result was that evangelism became a tarnished word. Only fanatics were evangelistic. The rest of us just wanted to enjoy *koinonia*, build our gyms, get rid of the JOY buses and have a good youth program. We turned inward with a vengeance.

Additionally, one cannot help but wonder about the long-range impact on Churches of Christ of the exodus to the Boston or Discipling Movement. Is it possible that we lost a generation of church planters and "soul winners"? While the "what if" game is a fruitless endeavor, one can still wonder. What would have been the impact if we had not lost even 20 gifted evangelists who could have started 20 large churches that started even more churches? If the experts are right in determining that only 10% of believers have the gift of evangelism, it would not take much of an exodus of these individuals to deplete the whole.

Theological issues have contributed to the demise of evangelism in our ranks as well. Much of our evangelistic activity in the past focused on converting members of denominational groups. We debated and dissected, converting many from other groups to "New Testament

Christianity." But now that many of us no longer view all of our denominational neighbors as "lost," we have lost our target audience and are having trouble figuring out what to do with evangelism. We incorrectly assume that everyone we meet has a church home, and perhaps we have subtly started to believe that, "Well, everybody is safe anyway." In most circles ecumenism can gather a crowd more quickly than evangelism. Honestly, what would you and I rather talk about: recognizing Christians in other groups or lost people going to hell?

Recently in a sermon I shared personal reflections about our heritage. Included was an admission that I did not believe we were "the only ones." The response was phenomenal as scores of members expressed similar feelings. "You said just what I have believed for years," was a common statement. It was a cathartic Sunday as many shed some unwanted baggage. But the challenge for my congregation and me is to move beyond this good feeling of, "Gee, isn't it nice to know we aren't the only ones." How do we want to spend the next 20 years—organizing pulpit swaps with the Baptists and Methodists or making real attempts to reach those outside of Christ?

We must reverse this inward focus and recover a sense of evangelism and mission. A recent experience illustrates this point. Philip Slate lectured to my congregation on tentmaking missions one Wednesday evening. He told several stories from the days when the Du Pont Company in Old Hickory, Tennessee, transferred employees to other regions of the country. Many of these employees used this opportunity to start new churches and strengthen small churches. Those who were scattered went everywhere preaching the gospel.[9] Following Slate's lecture I attended a going away party for one of our young families. They were being transferred to the Midwest. I had gone to some effort to find for them the largest Church of Christ in the area and had encouraged them to attend there. It never occurred to me to encourage them to view this as a mission opportunity. I had only thought of what was best for them and not what was best for the kingdom. My focus was internal only.

As we think about the kingdom and look at individual congregations, our emphasis on externals like praise teams or dramas on Sunday misses the point. The rhetoric of, "We have to move out of the rural 50s and join the twenty-first century," while true, is also deceptive. Singing new songs projected on a screen, telling the preacher to dress casually and dumping Sunday nights in favor of small groups may please the members under 50, but it will not make a church evangelistic. That change must come from within. As one minister of a new congregation has noted, "Many churches focus on externals. But what I have found is most churches need a heart change."[10] The heart change is a heart for the lost.

Conclusion

What does the future hold? Even on those blue Mondays, I remember to place my ultimate confidence in the Lord and not in some church growth strategy. But it also helps to remember the brethren I have known. I remember the man who went to the Atlantic coast with Du Pont fifty years ago and started numerous churches. And then there is my great uncle, dead before I was born. He worked for the railroad, preached on the weekends and vacations and somewhere along the way baptized my mother and her siblings. I remember the Gen X kid who never fit in and is now doing mission work in the Ukraine. I laugh with joy at the memory of a former co-worker who struggled with our traditions, bucked authority and yet remains committed to our fellowship and connects in an amazing way with teenagers today. I observe the passion of the millennial children in the youth group and marvel. I remember that two-hour long baptism service and think, "These are kids who will make a difference." Conversations with the Boomer elder who is retiring early to serve the church in a full-time voluntary capacity restores confidence in my maligned generation. I know that the hearts of many are hearts that long for the Lord and his church.

The future—the future is as bright as the promises of God.

Notes

1. Some of the significant decline among the Disciples can be attributed to a cleaning of the church roles over the last twenty years. In other words, the reported numbers for the Disciples in the 1950-70s were too high. Mainline churches do not include the Southern Baptists, who have experienced overall growth in the last quarter century.

2. Mac Lynn, *Churches of Christ in the United States* (Nashville: 21st Century Christian, 2000), 19-23.

3. William Strauss and Neil Howe, *Generations: The History of America's Future, 1584-2069* (New York: William Morrow, 1991).

4. The plethora of churches in a place like Nashville obviously contributes to this phenomenon. This changing of congregations is dominated by but not restricted to boomers.

5. Interview with Brad Small. This church planted in 1996 is called The Body of Christ at Amarillo South. The *Christian Chronicle* also covered the community church trend in March and April 2000. These articles are archived on their website, Christianchronicle.org.

6. This is not to imply that church planting is easy because it is not. Talented entrepreneur-type leaders are needed and the mortality rate is high. A leader of a hugely successful community church told me, "Twelve churches started the same year we did ten years ago. We are the only one in existence today." Denominations that offer training and support staff would not report such a high mortality rate among their church plants.

7. Interview with Jamey Miller, Christ Fellowship, Southlake, Texas. Miller does not claim unbridled success and notes that three other plants have not been successful.

8. The relocated church has been more up and down in attendance than the other three. Current attendance, however, is no higher than it was in 1986.

9. Slate tells the DuPont story in "DuPont's Old Hickory Employee Movement and the Spread of Churches of Christ: A Footnote in the Geography of Religion and Church Vitality," *Restoration Quarterly* (3rd Quarter 1997), 155-174.

10. Interview with Brad Small, Amarillo South.

———————————— Mission

11

The Church that Connects at Calvary

Mark Love

Crystal invited her neighbor to a Sunday evening "Coffee House," an explicitly evangelistic event our congregation hosts once a quarter. Her neighbor's response highlights the dilemma faced by many churches searching for the point of convergence between gospel and culture. "I'm not much interested in that," her neighbor responded, "but if you had something that would help me and my husband communicate better, I'd come to that." What does the church do? Does the church continue to talk past this woman with the unique language of salvation central to the faith? Or does the church "connect" with the woman by hosting a seminar on reflective listening, hoping to get her one step closer to the influence of the gospel? What are the terms of discourse between the church and the culture?

In past years the church could assume enough common terrain with the culture to speak in the distinctive vocabulary and cadences of the Christian faith. Direct evangelistic strategies like campaigns or gospel meetings proceeded on the assumption that we all spoke the same basic language. As Brian Smith suggests, "From the church's point of view, many of the sheep may be lost to the fold, but at least they knew there was a fold and had some idea of what it meant to be 'lost.'"[1]

Clearly, we no longer live in such a world. We live in a time of seismic transition. Our culture is described variously as post-Christian and postmodern, which means at the very least that we are not doing evangelism in Kansas anymore, Toto. We occupy a different world, one in which we are viewed increasingly as strangers speaking an odd language, practicing odd rituals.

There are two tendencies groups exhibit during transition. One tendency is to circle the wagons around the particularities of the faith for the purpose of preservation. This way a group knows who is in and who is out and preserves the distinctiveness of the faith no matter how out of step it is with the culture at large. While this approach keeps the enemy out of the camp, it tends not to be overtly missional. The second tendency is to go native, to learn to speak the language of the dominant culture so that we can carry on a meaningful conversation. This option encourages the translation of the faith into terms and concepts that speak more immediately to "seekers."[2] Relevance becomes the filter through which the church sifts evangelistic strategies. Given the dramatic shifts in our culture that seem to make the church's relevance less obvious, most who take mission seriously see the option of translation as the only responsible course of action. Moreover, given the impressive results of seeker churches like Willow Creek and Saddleback, the pull to mimic their direction is nearly irresistible. It seems to many to be the only viable option in our current circumstance.

One need only read the classified ads of churches looking for ministers in the *Christian Chronicle* to see the influence of seeker models on our thinking about evangelism. Churches now are seeking purpose-driven ministers to work with congregations featuring contemporary worship. We hold seminars to help churches connect. We study the habits and tastes of boomers, busters and X-ers hoping to offer a relevant word. We are enamored with the tantalizing promise of translation strategies.

While few would suggest that the circle-the-wagons approach is missionally superior to the go-native approach, the latter tack has its drawbacks as well. Smith sounds the alarm when he writes:

> For all its attractiveness, however, the road of translation is a broad way that leads to destruction, the destruction of the gospel. Translation inevitably means that the cultural particularities of the faith are viewed as secondary, perhaps even dispensable. In the interests of accessibility, the peculiar language and culture of the gospel are smoothed away in favor of existing conceptualities. The end result is a reductionism that transforms the gospel into the truisms of its hearers, and the Christian message is served up on the platters of the commonplace.[3]

While Smith's critique seems overly harsh, a clear risk of the translation option is the watering down of the gospel. We seem stuck with the lesser of two evils: the evil of irrelevance featured in the circle-the-wagons approach or the evil of syncretism featured in the go-native approach.

This dilemma is nothing new and the church has argued the merits of both positions throughout its history. We can see two distinct approaches to the point of convergence between gospel and culture even among the Gospels. Luke and John both seem to be interested in communicating to Hellenistic audiences. It is interesting at this point to note Luke's choice to stay within the grooves and contours of the story of Israel. He uses the language of Zion, or the primary religious and cultural vocabulary of Israel, to communicate the gospel to outsiders. John, however, chooses the more aggressive strategy of translation. John's gospel traffics in language more familiar to the receptor culture, clearly interested in making the gospel's unique claims accessible and immediately relevant to a Hellenistic sensibility.

This conversation has been repeated several times throughout church history, notably in the days of the apologists and in modern conversations of the recent past. Contrast Origen, for whom Plato was for the Greeks what Moses was for the Jews—a schoolmaster to bring the Hellenic mind to Christ, with Tertullian, whose well-known brusque protest to such an approach argues for the particular language and idiom of the Christian faith: "What has Athens to do with Jerusalem?... Away with all attempts to produce a mottled Christianity of Stoic,

Platonic, and dialectic composition." In modern conversations Paul Tillich can be heard speaking in an Alexandrian accent as he talks about strategies of "correlation" whereby the symbols of the ancient faith become relevant to modern listeners. On the other side, Karl Barth would suggest that not only do humans not know the right answers, they cannot form the proper questions unless they are encountered by God.

This brief foray into history is designed to back two observations. First, the conversation is unavoidable and legitimate, and the church will always be defining evangelism somewhere within the tension of these perspectives. Those who speak the language of Zion will need to find someplace to stand in the marketplace to be heard. Those who translate will always struggle with how to teach seekers the distinctive language and practices of the faith. Second, and more importantly for my essay, the translation approach pursued so single-mindedly by so many in our churches is part of a theological legacy that carries certain assumptions and risks. Beyond the irony of Hybels and Warren sharing a bed with Origen and Tillich, it should be pointed out that John's gospel required a follow-up set of letters to check heretical abuses of those using John's Gospel for support. Pick a heretic of the first few centuries and odds are they list John as their favorite gospel. Moreover, the Alexandrian program of Origen ultimately led him to be repudiated and condemned by the church. The risks of approaches relying too heavily on translation are not minor and such approaches should not be undertaken lightly.

I would like to suggest an approach to evangelism, practiced by the East County Church of Christ, that takes a more direct approach with regard to the gospel without giving up the quest for relevance. It may represent something of a middle way that allows the gospel to speak to the culture on the gospel's terms but in a way that demonstrates a cruciform relevance.

Gospel on its Own Terms

East County's journey into a more meaningful approach to evangelism began with revisiting the notion of gospel. Practically speaking, the gospel had been circumscribed or granted only a limited relevance. The gospel had been reduced to a message, often under the banner "plan of salvation," relevant only to securing a home in heaven. Given such a limited relevance, it is quite natural for churches to meet outsiders "where they live" and bring them gradually to a place where they can hear the specifics of the plan of salvation. In this scheme, the flow of discourse begins with the presenting issues of the culture from which the church hopes to gain a hearing for a message about eternal salvation. This approach is reductionist with regard to the gospel, and apologetic with regard to the culture.

It is true that the gospel can be reduced to simple terms (although I think we are often confused about what it means to preach a "simple gospel"). I would suggest that the gospel can be reduced to the announcement of an event—the death, burial and resurrection of Jesus (cf. 1 Cor 15:1-11; Acts 2:22-24; 10:34-53). God has acted in the death and resurrection of Jesus for the salvation of the world. The gospel, at its most basic level, is the announcement of an event that has significance for all humankind. Notice that it is reducible to the announcement of an *event*. It is not reducible to a single message, telling, or interpretation of the event. The gospel cannot be reduced to a single theory of the atonement, to an explication of the trinity or even to the plan of salvation. These are faulty reductions that move the simplicity of the gospel in the wrong direction. Moreover, the event-announcement character of the gospel is vital to its remaining precisely that—good news. This point will be developed more fully below. For now, let us note that the gospel is reducible to the announcement of the death, burial and resurrection of Jesus and it is assumed to be relevant to all: "We are convinced that one has died for all" (2 Cor. 5:14).

While the event of the cross is the rudiment of the gospel, it is also the surpassing wisdom of God. Though it is a sparse outline, it is also an encompassing logic. The event of the cross issues forth in a word, that is a *logos* or logic, which takes every thought captive. So for Paul, "The word (*logos*) of the cross is foolishness to those who are perishing, but to those who are being saved it is the power of God" (1 Cor.

1:18). At this point the gospel is expansive and expressive. No one metaphor, image or outcome can exhaust its meanings. Terms like redemption, justification, sanctification and reconciliation intersect the continuum of relevance at various points—bondage, guilt, alienation, emptiness or despair, to name but a few. When the images and meanings of the cross begin to be explored and plumbed, the church is able to initiate more "relevant" conversations with the culture on the gospel's own terms.

The pervasiveness of this logic, at least for Paul, cannot be overstated. Paul's self-understanding in relation to the death and resurrection of Jesus is profound. He can say things like, "I am crucified with Christ, nevertheless I live, yet not I but Christ who lives in me," or "I want to know Christ and the power of his rising, share in his sufferings, conform to his death," or "While we live we are always being given up to death for Jesus' sake, so that the life of Jesus might be made visible in our mortal flesh" (Gal. 2:19-20; Phil. 3:10; 2 Cor 4:11). He has become a gospeled person, a rendering of the death and resurrection itself. This self-identification is thoroughgoing. When Paul says to the Corinthians, "I decided to know nothing among you except Christ and him crucified" (1 Cor 2:2), he is not referring to the message or words he is preaching, but to the very manner of his preaching—his preaching style—which is willing to locate strength in weakness. I find Galatians 3:1 an intriguing text in this regard: "You foolish Galatians! Who has bewitched you? It was before your eyes that Jesus Christ was publicly exhibited as crucified!" When was this? How was this? I think Paul is pointing directly to the style of his ministry. "I am crucified with Christ…" (2:20).

This leads me to another important aspect of understanding the notion of gospel. It cannot be captured by a message. Though the event of the cross always issues forth in a word or a *logos*, it can never be completely expressed by that word. Many have noted the various and diverse ways gospel is expressed as a message in the New Testament. It is overly simplistic to equate the synoptic formula "good news of the kingdom" with Paul's notions of new creation. They are not mere synonyms. However, they are expressions, interpretations or contextualizations of a common event. Though their syntax and idiom may vary, they share certain features in common that allow them to fly under the banner of gospel.

Let me say it this way. The gospel is a phenomenon. It is a word-event, in the best Hebrew sense of that notion, that has certain observable characteristics. The gospel has certain instincts, postures and rhythms that make it powerful, active and converting. I think this is seen in Paul's statement in 1 Thessalonians when he writes, "the gospel happened[4] among you not in word only, but also in power and in the Holy Spirit and with full conviction" (1:4-5). The gospel is manifest not only in a message, but also in human life, in forms and strategies, and in real human communities living under the announcement of the death and resurrection of Jesus. In this sense, as Beaudean suggests, "the gospel is therefore something of a saving dynamic environment."[5]

The gospel not only wants to say something, it wants to act a certain way. The gospel is not only the announcement of an event, it is the very extension or manifestation of that announcement. It seeks to reenact the drama of the death and resurrection of Jesus in every human circumstance. In this sense, the gospel is always seeking relevance on its own terms.

What are the observable characteristics of the gospel? Let's begin with the very word gospel. James Brownson points out that "gospel" was not the only available term to denote the Christian message.[6] The term gospel carries with it specific connotations which in turn produce meanings and behaviors. For instance, gospel is public declaration. It is news. It cannot simply be mapped on to existing conceptualities. The gospel's first instinct is not apologetic but pronouncement. The gospel is not a dressed up wisdom or an improvement on human wisdom up to this point. It is the startling announcement that a new order is emerging with an alternative wisdom, embodied in the death and resurrection of Jesus. The gospel's first interest is not to create common ground but to reveal new ground. On this new ground the gospel calls for nothing less than repentance and demands conversion. The gospel is news.

I would also suggest that gospel is a narrative category. It is best understood, not as a series of propositions, but as an event that culminates a story. As Paul suggests, Jesus died in accordance with the scriptures (1 Cor 15:3-4). While scripture includes many forms or genres of literature, the overall narrative shape and scope of scripture is undeniable and vital for the establishment of faith. As Stanley Hauerwas reminds:

> The fact that we come to know God through the recounting of the story of Israel and the life of Jesus is decisive for our understanding of the kind of God we worship as well as the world in which we exist....Narrative is not secondary for our knowledge of God; there is no "point" that can be separated from the story. The narratives through which we learn of God are the point.[7]

The gospel is truest to its own instincts when it draws listeners into relationship with God through the recounting of his mighty acts in history. Walter Brueggemann captures this narrative thrust when he suggests that "evangelism means inviting people into these stories as the definitional stories of our life, and thereby authorizing people to give up, abandon and renounce other stories that have shaped their lives in false and distorting ways."[8] Conversion occurs not through the mastery of a certain set of facts or propositions, but through participation in a drama that calls for particular habits and new allegiances. Telling the Christian story, whether in recital or testimony, is the preferred speech of evangelism.

The phenomenon of gospel is also observed in relation to the event announced—the death and resurrection of Jesus. In other words, the death of Jesus reveals the character of God, and so makes visible the way God carries himself in the world. This way does not lord it over others, quench smoldering wicks, or lift up its voice in the streets. Rather, the witness of the gospel comes in humility, in counting others better than oneself, and through plain speech by the open statement of the truth.

I have tried to make the case that the gospel is a phenomenon that has certain observable characteristics. Subsequently, the gospel has certain instincts and always hopes to speak in ways in keeping with its own logic and personality. I think Juan Louis Segundo has something of this in mind when he proposes a "hermeneutic" for evangelism. For the church to be true to the interests of the gospel, Segundo suggests communicating only the essentials of the Christian message, communicating it as good news, and adding nothing further except at a pace that will allow the essential element to remain essentially that.[9] Segundo's proposal deserves further exploration, but let me say at this point only that it is an effort to allow the gospel itself to be the starting place for conversation with the larger culture.

At East County we have taken a broader tack in understanding the gospel as a phenomenon. We have listed seven characteristics of gospel that serve as guidelines for evangelism. Evangelism at East County is:

1. *Cross-focused*. Every evangelistic strategy we employ proceeds from a word of the cross.
2. *Direct*. We will first let the gospel have its own say. While apologetics may have its place in discourse with outsiders, it is not first-order gospel discourse. The gospel is news that has no analogous reality.
3. *Narrative*. Moving away from propositional approaches to evangelism, we seek to convey the dramatic movement of the redemptive story as it appears in scripture, the life of God's people, and the life of the listener.
4. *Community Coherent*. By this we mean that as validation of our message we will point to the realities of an intentional, counter-cultural community. People in a postmodern age will be less and less impressed with fine sounding arguments, and instead will look for the truth of the faith in the experience of an alternative community.
5. *Humble/confessional*. The cross not only informs our message, but posture. The judgment of the cross runs not only through the world, but also through the heart of the church.

6. *Passionate.* We share good news. Therefore, we share it joyfully and urgently.

7. *Conversational/Artistic.* If the gospel announces a world not made available by the rulers and principalities of this age, then evangelistic speech must be expressive and evocative. This kind of discourse is not monologue, but conversation that fuses the horizon of the gospel and the listener in powerful and suggestive ways.

While another list might serve the same purpose better, these guidelines represent an attempt to let the gospel speak on its own terms in our evangelistic ministry. We think we are not only being true to the gospel as a message, but to the gospel as a phenomenon. Moreover, as we become more fluent in the logic of the cross, we are learning that it is powerful to save and immediately relevant on its own terms. This restores the church's confidence in the initiative of God in bringing people to salvation. With the recovery of an active God, the church feels empowered and liberated to join in the work of evangelism.

The Church as Gospel Hermeneutic

In the previous section I suggested that the gospel possesses a greater relevance on its own merits than our traditional understandings have allowed. Moreover, the gospel not only wants to say something, it wants to act a certain way. Understood as a phenomenon, the gospel hopes to act in a far more direct, revelatory way than most modern approaches to evangelism have allowed. I would like to deepen these observations by suggesting that the church, as an intentional community formed by the event of the death and resurrection of Jesus, and living by this event's unique logic, becomes the prism wherein the gospel's light refracts across the plane of human need and culture. Though the church may define itself over and against "the world" or the culture, the fact is that the church is always inescapably a cultural expression. Our members use computers, watch television, commute to work, read self-help books and daily newspapers. It seems a safer assumption that our members have been shaped by the culture and its wisdom more than they have by the distinctive logic of the death and resurrection of Jesus. Still, the church is also the community willing to place itself under the claims of the gospel. Ideally, the church is the arena in which the event of the gospel becomes a word—a relevant word. The church then is the hermeneutic for the gospel to the world. As George Hunsberger suggests, "We are present with them to provide the lens, the language by which they may grasp and be grasped by that same gospel...In the gospel's encounter with the culture, the gospel meets the culture first here in us, in an inner dialogue; similarly, the culture meets the gospel first here in us who are the hermeneutical lens through which it may be perceived."[10]

My sense is that our infatuation with seeker strategies has short-circuited the hermeneutical conversation necessary for the church to act in ways in keeping with the gospel. Opting for the quick seduction of consumer strategies, we have interrupted the "inner dialogue" Hunsberger speaks of and truncated the gospel's potential to speak a relevant word to the world on its own terms. Too often the culture's first experience with the church does not provide a gospel wisdom at all, but a wisdom already recognized by the culture. The argument typically given is that the church needs to demonstrate its relevance for everyday living before people will be willing to hear the gospel. Again, what I am arguing is that the logic of the cross is so pervasive and expansive that the church loses nothing to relevance by speaking on the gospel's terms.

Finding this cruciform relevance will require that the church live with single-minded resolve with regard to the death and resurrection of Jesus. The church must learn a gospeled existence, just as individual members learn what it means to see their lives through the lens of the death and resurrection. This is no quick fix. It demands the evangelization of the church.[11] As Brueggemann suggests, "evangelism is no safe church activity that will sustain a conventional church, nor a routine enterprise that will support a societal status quo."[12] The conversion demanded of the church, however, will lead to words which are both gospel and relevant.

Conclusion

In this time of seismic transition, we are tempted to think that radical translation strategies are our only responsible missional option. I am suggesting that before we truncate the gospel and grant it only a limited relevance, we determine to live more deeply in it as a phenomenon and pervasive logic. As Brownson writes,

> If we want to peel back the cultural accretions and clear off the barnacles of institutionalization and tradition, we do not need only a new kind of philosophical or cultural or historical analysis, as vital as those things might be (and I do think they are essential). What we need, at an even deeper level, is an encounter with the message of the cross that changes the frame of reference we use to make our way in the world.[13]

A lesbian hears the gospel for the first time. Her whole existence has been shaped by her sexual identity and the issue of whether or not this orientation is biological or learned. As a Christian, living intentionally in the logic of the cross, those issues are no longer relevant. Daily she cedes her identity, her entire identity, over to God with the belief and hope that he can raise her up whole and complete. She has a new kind of wisdom that goes beyond the discussions of nature or nurture. For her the gospel is immediately relevant to issues of sexual identity. The church is also learning from this wisdom. Heterosexual males are also learning that their sexual identity is not an end in itself, but must be given over to the lordship of Jesus.

A husband lives with his new wife even though shortly after their marriage she refuses to have anything to do with him. His "Christian" counselor tells him to divorce her. How can he expect to be fulfilled if his wife is unwilling to give him the things he needs? This man, however, has released his wife from the burden of having to meet all his needs. He is counting on the promise of the gospel—that in plenty or in want Christ is sufficient for all our needs. Far from being a doormat or a victim in this relationship, he is learning of the power of the reconciling love of God. He is being transformed through his keeping of covenant, and through the hope of the gospel that she is being changed by a love given without expecting anything in return. This is death and resurrection love, a unique wisdom that the rest of the church is learning to apply to marriage.[14]

A church is learning that the conventional wisdom about boundaries is not particularly Christian. While issues of codependency in a relationship are significant, many of the solutions offered by our therapeutic culture are rooted in the Western myth of the autonomous individual. Christian discipleship calls us to lose our lives in order to find them, or to use Paul's language, to offer our lives as living sacrifices. We are not called to construct and maintain our own identities through establishing boundaries, but to receive our selves in relation to the call of the kingdom. This is pretty boundaryless language and can lead to a fairly exposed existence. The risks of boundaryless living can only be chosen within a community that has different notions of power and significance than those the world professes—notions rooted in the death and resurrection of Jesus.[15]

It is in the midst of moving deeper into the significance of the gospel that the church finds its voice and learns it has something to say to the culture around it. I would hope that we would have a *logos*, a word of the cross, for Crystal's friend the next time she is approached with the announcement of good news. "We have something better than listening skills. Through the good news of Jesus we have discovered a way of viewing the world that transforms us and will make both of you different people, even different listeners. The death and resurrection of Jesus will leave no aspect of your life unchanged." Let those with ears to hear receive the good news.

Notes

1. Brian K. Smith, "Christianity as a Second Language: Rethinking Mission in the West," *Theology Today* (January, 1997), 443.

2. I am aware that the word translation is somewhat problematic at this point. I certainly don't want to suggest that the gospel has some official lan-

guage or has some pure distillation that can be abstracted from cultural expression. In this sense, the gospel is always translatable. I use translation the way Smith does in his article, as a strategy to begin the conversation with the culture on the culture's terms.

3. Smith, 444.

4. *To euanggelion hemon egenethe eis humas.* I am following the translation of John William Beaudean, Jr., *Paul's Theology of Preaching*, NABPR Dissertation Series, Number 6 (Macon, GA: Mercer University Press, 1988), 36.

5. Beaudean, 56.

6. "In articulating the essential character of its faith, early Christianity could have adopted one of the terms commonly used in the Hellenistic religious world such as 'illumination' (*photismos*) or 'knowledge' (*gnosis*), or 'mystery' (*mysterion*)." James V. Brownson, "Speaking the Truth in Love," *The Church Between Gospel and Culture*, George Hunsberger, Craig Van Gelder, eds. (Grand Rapids, MI: Eerdmans, 1996), 250-251.

7. Stanley Hauerwas, *The Peaceable Kingdom* (South Bend, IN: Notre Dame University, 1983), 25.

8. Walter Brueggemann, *Biblical Perspectives on Evangelism: Living in a Three-Storied Universe* (Nashville: Abingdon, 1993), 10.

9. Juan Luis Segundo, *The Liberation of Theology* (Maryknoll, NY: Orbis, 1976), 8.

10. George Hunsberger, "Acquiring the Posture of a Missionary Church," *The Church Between Gospel and Culture*, 296-297. Hunsberger is following here the influential lead of Lesslie Newbigin, *The Gospel in a Pluralist Society* (Grand Rapids, MI: Eerdmans, 1988) 222-223.

11. See Darrell L. Gruder, *The Continuing Conversion of the Church* (Grand Rapids, MI: Eerdmans, 2000).

12. Brueggemann, 129.

13. Brownson, "Hearing the Gospel Again, for the First Time," *Confident Witness, Changing World: Rediscovering the Gospel in North America* (Grand Rapids, MI: Eerdmans, 1999), 134.

14. It seems to me that this is a radically different approach than what is commonly offered as Christian advice on marriage. Often couples are taught to think of marriage as an economic exchange, a *quid pro quo* kind of arrangement, where a mutual satisfying of a hierarchy of needs is being accomplished. This approach might work and still be less than Christian. It is contractual and not covenantal. Moreover, gospeled husbands and wives might discover that their hierarchy of needs is being reshuffled.

15. See Shelley Neilson's perceptive article, "With the Affection of Christ: A Pauline Model for Relationships in Ministry," *Leaven* 5 (Summer 1997), 4-8.

12

A Place for the Lonely

Kevin Wooten

He came to our campus ministry with a friend, but Brett was obviously a misfit, one of the guys no guy wants to be around for very long. He was a bit clumsy, a little loud and shy on social skills. Though he was highly intelligent, his first semester GPA was less than 1.0 due to a lack of discipline, so he was on academic probation. I learned enough about his home life to realize he was a misfit there too. He was yelled at, blamed, corrected and generally made to feel unwanted. To sum it up, Brett was pretty much alone.

Campus ministries often attract students like Brett. He found a few people who genuinely cared about him. They invited him to lunch after church. They asked him to see a movie. He went with us on weekend trips and to weekly Bible studies and campouts. He rarely missed an event because he had found a place to be loved and to be somebody.

Prior to our annual fall trek to Lake Cumberland for a weekend retreat, Brett had been talking more seriously to a couple of closer friends about Jesus' desire to be the Lord of our lives. At our retreat he decided that's what he wanted for his life. In the most precious and innocent conversation I've ever had with someone, I asked him why he was making this choice. From the very core of his heart he replied, "I don't want to be alone anymore." I can't tell you how many times

I've heard those words of his echo in my own heart. I truly believe Brett hit the sentiment of many young people right at the core: they don't want to be alone anymore.

Lonely people have been searching for God since the beginning of time. I don't know if people's hearts are more lonely in the twenty-first century than in the past. All I know is that I certainly see it in the faces of students on college campuses. Maybe loneliness is more pronounced because of the rise in divorce rates or the greater numbers of absentee parents. Maybe loneliness is more prominent due to the way we have tried to supplant the number of hours spent with children with the number of dollars spent on children. I wonder if the blending of families is a factor. Two single parents decide to get together and their children now become brothers and sisters. How much say do the children have about this new arrangement? What does having a stranger as a brother do to them? Does their powerlessness produce a feeling of not really counting for much? I don't know exactly what precipitates the loneliness, but I do know it's draining life from young hearts.

What does the wing of God's Kingdom identified as Churches of Christ offer to lonely people? Brett's words about not being alone anymore had nothing to do with a blank daytimer. It had little to do with having friends. His words had everything to do with realizing God's presence in his life. Jesus met a woman like Brett one day. She too seemed to be a misfit. She had few friends, a string of husbands and a heart longing to be filled. She asked Jesus where she could find God. She was tired of being alone. Jesus gave her a timeless answer which had zero to do with small groups or Sunday school or doctrine. He put her on a path called worship—a path that leads to the throneroom of our King (John 4:1-26). Jesus says to her in essence, "A time is coming and is already here when people like yourself may find God wherever you are because God is spirit and worship is spiritual. So wherever you may be you are within reach of God's hand. You are invited to step right through the doors of God's throneroom, right into His presence." In the presence of the King, the nagging edge of loneliness is dulled a bit. We may still get yelled at. We may still get laughed at. We may still be misunderstood. We may still be misfits. Yet because we live in God's presence daily, the drain of loneliness won't sap us dry.

Our God is Real

Worship seems to be God's answer to most of what ails us, not just loneliness. Perhaps God keeps pointing us to worship because worship brings Him to life. More than anything else in my life, I need to know that God is real. Paul tells us that when an unbeliever walks into our worship assembly he needs to be undoubtedly convinced that God is really among us (1 Cor. 14:24-25).

When I first entered vocational ministry fourteen years ago, I thought effective worship was related to pulling different strings. I thought we needed to change the window display, rearrange the shelves, dress up the salespeople. Over the past few years many stylistic changes have occurred in our worship assemblies, but in time those too will become routine and yet another generation will clamor for change. Even though pulling different strings does not guarantee God will be made real to us, change is inevitable and the church is definitely not immune. People think differently, have different experiences and consequently different worldviews than 20 years ago. So changes in style need to occur thoughtfully, intentionally and prayerfully.

Beware, however, of believing that cutting-edge worship style equals effective worship. We live in a culture that places a high value on being entertained. Elmo and Big Bird taught those now in their twenties and early thirties how to read. The Super Bowl is more about the multi-million-dollar commercials than the game. Teaching without PowerPoint makes me a dinosaur. We want to be titillated. We want extreme games. We want never-before-seen special effects. Then we come and sit in a pew on Sunday morning waiting to see if God is real. Will He perform for us? Will He entertain us? Just like Elijah, we may be looking for Him in the spectacular, yet He speaks to us in a whisper. Maybe "surroundsound," concert highs and thrill rides chase away the loneliness for a moment. Maybe we want life to be roaring and revving to drown out the pain. Maybe our worship times at church are more comfortable with professionals performing for an audience.

Maybe that's why we had rather worship in an auditorium than a sanctuary. Maybe getting quiet enough to hear the whisper is just too deafening.

What we need is to allow God to wrap His huge arms around us and listen to Him sing a love song to us. What we do instead is try to wrap our arms around God and tell Him how to behave. Maybe we have lost our sense of imagination in our quest to be entertained. When I was a kid, I drove GI Joe around in mom's shoes alongside my neighbor's Barbie. A high heeled shoe was a jacked-up Chevy Super Sport. A flat shoe was the Gremlin GI kept in the garage. We had great imaginations. Yet my imagination was nothing like my parent's imagination. They really believe they walked uphill both ways on their daily fifty-mile trek to school. And to top it off, they imagined I believed their story. My children don't have to imagine much. They just pop in a Dreamcast game and they have a three-dimensional obstacle course to navigate with a 400 HP cigar boat. I haven't even mentioned Barney. Parental storytelling has been ousted by a purple dinosaur.

Honor the Mystery of God

What we're allowing to happen is dangerous when it comes to our perception of God. When we take away the mystery of God, He immediately becomes limited to the confines of our own minds. Nowhere are we asked by God to put our arms around Him. We would have to shrink Him down to near impotence to hold Him. I heard someone talk of how they lost their love for the Lord when their faith became a system to be defended rather than a power to be experienced. Where is the mystery of God? Are we okay with unanswered questions? We honestly think sometimes that God will be more real if we could just gain more knowledge. But without mystery, there will be no worship. Without mystery, there will be nothing but self-sufficiency. Without mystery, God becomes someone we thank for what He began some time ago but which we are now completing on our own.

Do you remember Job's demand for God to meet Him in the courtroom? Job had let go of the mystery of God and he was feeling very much alone. Job shouted, "I have my rights!" which is not much of a mystery-filled proclamation. Then God answers questions Job really didn't ask and this time God speaks out of a storm, not a whisper. For 129 verses God says to Job, "Don't you dare try to corner me! Don't you dare try to put your puny little arms around me!" Perhaps the main statement God drills Job with is this: "Brace yourself like a man; I will question you, and you shall answer me" (Job 40:7). Job's response is a classic worship response. He acknowledges that God is real: "My ears had heard you but now my eyes have seen you" (42:5). He acknowledges that God is mysterious: "Surely I spoke of things I did not understand, things too wonderful for me" (42:3). Then Job repents, a fairly common occurrence when God becomes real to someone (42:6).

Don't we want a God who is larger than we are? Do we want to worship a God we can explain or manipulate? Someone my size isn't going to be much help with the size problems I have. I want to be drawn up into the throneroom of a King who is larger than my needs and your needs combined. I want to be changed by His holiness. He is the One who needs to speak in worship, not me. I need to listen, celebrate the mystery and repent.

Storytelling may be one of the doors through which we gain access to the throneroom. Storytelling honors the mystery of God's work in people's lives. We love to hear stories, real people's stories. Surely the people of God have a powerful story to tell. Several months ago on a Sunday morning one of our best storytellers was preaching. My seat was directly across from the high school students, so I was able to watch their faces and responses easily. Jim, the storyteller, was on a roll, sharing one of his life's best stories. For fifteen minutes not a single one of those thirty teenagers moved a muscle. Their eyes were glued onto Jim. He had them in his back pocket for fifteen solid minutes. Then he said these words: "Now, let me give you a couple of applications." Guess what? The countenance of nearly 30 high schoolers changed, as it did for many of us older folks too. They took their eyes off Jim and started looking around. They began to fidget and started to grab for stuff. They may have still been listening, but I know it was harder for them to hear.

In our pews sit scores of people and each one has a story—a story of faith, a story of growth, a story of struggle, a story of victory, a story of joy, a story the King has authored. Those stories help make a distant and invisible God real. When the throneroom is filled with real people with real stories about a real and living God—well, the throneroom becomes a safe place. We desperately need a continual flow of real people's stories. Stories of brokenness like Isaiah, of rebellion like Jonah, of courage like Daniel, of determination like Nehemiah, of repentance like David, of commitment like Stephen, of boldness like Esther, of humility like Mary. In placing the stories of how God has led us alongside the recorded stories of people in the Bible, the throneroom doors again will be flung open, letting anyone who is seeking know she is welcome here.

No story is too awful or too far along for God to take charge of it and to fill it with His grace. But if people don't hear the stories from those sitting around them, they might begin to believe their story is hopeless—and that's an overwhelming feeling of loneliness, again. Remember the words, "I don't want to feel alone anymore"? Our stories make for real worship of a real God who keeps real promises. As this song says:

> God will make a way where there seems to be no way,
> He works in ways we cannot see,
> He will make a way for me.
> He will be my guide,
> Hold me closely to His side,
> With love and grace for each new day,
> He will make a way, He will make a way.

Stories soften our hearts for God to speak to us, whether in a shout or a whisper. Every time we hear Him, He becomes a little more real to us. Maybe this is why God has chosen to reveal Himself to us primarily through the stories of His people. Maybe this is why Jesus used stories to teach us how to follow Him. Stories of faith honor a God who is alive and who is active in ways we would never dream of ourselves.

A Place for the Lonely

Stories of faith are always about how great God is and how gifted we are to live in His presence daily.

Music, as well as storytelling, may be another door to God's throneroom. Music has always been the language of the heart. If we took all the music and people stories out of our Bibles, they would become much thinner. Music is a language God has used since the beginning of time to connect with the heart of His creation and to tell us of His greatness.

Listen to the words of this song. The author reminds us not only of God's size, but also that He'll never leave us.

> I am a sheep and the Lord is my Shepherd;
> Watching over my soul!
> My soul to keep guarding over me ever;
> Watching wherever I go!
> And when the winds blow;
> He is my shelter!
> And when I'm lost and alone He rescues me!
> And when the lion comes He is my victory!
> Constantly watching over me!

Remember Brett's words, "I don't want to be alone anymore"? That song speaks to the heart of a lonely person. God invites us to crawl up in His lap and be soothed and calmed by His love.

> Day by day,
> You reveal Your love to me.
> Cradled in Your arms I am a precious lamb;
> A diamond in Your eyes.

We need that song and many others. Those words soften us so we can hear what the King has to say from His throneroom.

God is using music to draw people to Jesus. Thirty minutes from my house over fifty thousand young people gathered for four days to hear music. And it was all about God. On May 20, 2000, at Shelby Farms in

Memphis sixty thousand university students came together for one day to fast, pray and praise. Music helped draw them there. We need to be weaving new songs into our worship times. Some of these songs may be conducive to congregational singing. Some may be more conducive to simply being heard. In either situation, worship happens. We are drawn a little closer to God.

This past semester we planned late-evening Sunday night worship times for college students. Music was a big part of our worship. We sang to each other; we sang with each other; we listened to other people's music; we even sang an old song from Hee Haw one night. During our worship in song I saw smiles, laughter, tears, eyes closed, eyes looking up, hands raised, hands holding other hands. Music which speaks from our hearts and to our hearts will make a powerful statement about the reality of God's presence in our lives.

Revive Our Memory

In addition to honoring the mystery of God, I believe a strong memory will also help us to know God is real. First, we need to remember where we have come from. In Paul's letters, he never lets us forget his past. Or maybe he's recalling his past for his own benefit. Maybe he doesn't ever want to forget where and what he used to be. Our past experiences and sins should never stop us from growing and some memories would be better left forgotten, but the reality of past lostness must never escape our memory. The moment we forget what and where we were, that's the same moment we lose touch with God's grace. When we forget that we depend on grace, we don't need God to be real.

Paul did not write those memories of the past just to be humble. He relived the hopelessness of his life without a Savior. He drew power from his conversion memories to keep on going. I can hear Paul thinking as he's being beaten again, "God got me in this; he can surely get me through it!"

Do you remember being lost? Are you able to experience again the joy of your salvation? Reliving and retelling the story of how and where God found you will empower your worship and make God real to you again. Our lostness must forever remain in our memories, not for the purpose of weighing us down, but for honoring the miraculous work of God through Jesus Christ and for believing that we will never be alone again.

In Churches of Christ, we have another great tradition where spiritual renewal flows through remembering. Every Sunday we participate in the Lord's Supper, an event Jesus said to do in His memory. Memory for us usually means thinking back to a time when…but Jesus is advocating a somewhat different idea than just thinking back.

For example, I can easily think back to my first cross country meet as a freshmen in high school. Our coach had been trained by General Patton himself. He made Sargeant Carter look like a wimp. He yelled. He ridiculed. He intimidated. He challenged us to fight him. And we won most every meet. Near the end of my first race, I was in serious pain. I could be heard gasping loudly for every breath of air. I sounded like some large mammal in the throes of labor. Finally I crossed the finish line, nowhere near the front of the pack, stopped running, bent over and heaved anything that would come out of my guts. I thought I was going to die. About an hour later in our coach's post-race ridiculing session, he began telling everybody about my finish—the gasps, the pain, the hurling. I didn't really care to rehash the situation, but he didn't ask me. Then, in a totally unexpected move, he said, "Wooten's the only one who ran hard today. I expect every single one of you to puke after every single race. (Long pause.) Nice race, Kevin." In a sick sort of way, I was a bit proud. However I didn't look forward to the next race.

In the past several years I have run lots of other races, from 5K's to marathons. Sometimes it hurts to run. When the pain hits I keep running and sometimes I remember my coach's message to me. I remember that pain is not necessarily a good reason to quit and I remember that if you want to be your best you're going to have to hurt. The power of that memory has been brought forward to the present many times and in many situations in my life.

I believe that's what Jesus had in mind when he said, "Do this in my memory." As the Jewish people celebrated Passover, they did not simply participate in a sentimental recollection. They re-experienced the power of that past deliverance out of Egypt and brought confidence into their present situation that God is still their Deliverer. God asked us to proclaim Jesus' death until He comes whenever we participate in communion. We obey that command as we bring the power of Jesus' crucifixion and resurrection into our present situation where God's resurrection power may again make a life-changing difference. Then Jesus living in me becomes reality. The intent of the Lord's Supper is not to stroll down memory lane or to put us on a guilt trip because we put Jesus on the cross. The intent is for us to be revitalized by the reality of Christ's living body today and the continual flow of forgiveness in our lives through Christ's blood.

Continue to Meet Jesus

Mystery and memory both play a major role in our experience with God. But I believe this last principle helps make God more real than anything else I know. Back in 1981 when I was a junior at Western Kentucky University, we would pack around 100 students into a 600 square foot room on Friday nights. People were everywhere, and we sang. We sang every Stamps-Baxter tune ever written. We raised the roof with our enthusiastic voices. Our theme song was "Hilltops of Glory" because we were the WKU Hilltoppers. We would sing till we were hoarse. Then on Sunday morning we would go to church by the dozens, sit right up front, and sing our hearts out. Those were some great worship experiences. You know what, though? Those songs were not all that great. We did not have a worship team. The preaching—well let's say we became very tolerant and developed low expectations. But you could not have kept us students away. Why? Simply because we did not put any pressure on the Sunday morning worship service to change our lives.

This last principle focuses on meeting Jesus all week long. In that campus ministry we were talking about Jesus, praying in the mornings together, sharing our faith, studying the Bible with others, baptizing students. We were worshiping all week long. We were meeting Jesus in our conversations with others every day.

A Place for the Lonely

In junior high I joined the band and began playing the French horn. Band was great—for about six months. I recall three major turn-offs: practicing, concerts and Kim Porter. If not for those three things I would have stuck it out. Miss Porter was the biggest problem, though. She also played the French horn but she was not like me; she was good, and she knew it. She had good posture; I slumped. She never missed a note; I rarely nailed one. She had a thumb key on her horn; I didn't (but I did have some definite thoughts on what she could do with her thumb key). I was never very good and only got worse when I quit practicing on my own. I learned an important lesson from band. You never get any better if the only time you play is during concerts, and eventually you will dread those times.

The same is true for worship. If worship is not a way of life through the week, then Sunday will be forever disconnected and disappointing. Do you think the new community of believers we read about in Acts 2 got bored with their worship times? Did they ever think, "We're so tired of singing these same old songs of David. We need some new songs. And doesn't Peter have any other sermon than the one about Jesus and the cross. That's all we hear about!" Every day that passed the believers in that community worshiped. They didn't live with the pressure or expectation of having to adore God, study His word, listen to Him, acknowledge and confess their sins, be transformed, be resolved, receive peace, participate in the Lord's Supper, evangelize and equip, and catch what time the next potluck is all in the same time it takes for Lenscrafters to make a pair of glasses...that is, in just about an hour. Now that's pressure! Honestly, those expectations will never be met until we begin worshiping God and meeting Jesus all week long.

With every person God puts in our path, expect to meet Jesus. Every lonely person, every broken-hearted person, every poor person, every confused person, every lost person—just expect to meet Jesus in their eyes. If we do not see Jesus all week long, week after week, month after month, then we will not see Him on Sunday year after year. If God is going to be real to us in this new millennium then we must meet Him today.

Our Message is Relevant

Another major emphasis for this new millennium is that our message must be relevant. Listen to these words from a graduate student in political science:

> The last several months have been a huge adjustment for me. And while they have certainly been a time of growth, they have also been incredibly frustrating and really not very enjoyable at all....Political science at this level is a completely different subject than it is at the undergraduate level. No one seems to be concerned with anything that's really going on in the world, except as evidence for this or that theory. Prescriptive statements of any sort are automatically dismissed because of their normative overtones. Thus, there seems to be little purpose behind what we're doing. It's appropriate that our department is on the twelfth, thirteenth and fourteenth floors of the social science building—this image of an ivory tower presents itself quite easily.[1]

The key line in that letter is, "There seems to be little purpose in what we're doing." In the year 2000 so many options are available for how we may spend our time that settling for just going to church because the doors are open is history. Churches have been recreating Sunday nights because of this reality. Now more than ever before we must face the question—what is the purpose of this event and what difference will it make in people's lives?

Time has become one of life's most valuable commodities. We simply do not have time to waste. We do not have time to go sit in a worship service which leaves us feeling as empty as we were when we arrived. As you can guess, traditions have lost their staying power over the past few years. Denominational loyalty has also dissipated. Relevancy is the reason. If traditions are not making a difference in what I deal with on Monday at work or Tuesday night at home then I will not make time to honor them. I will use my limited and valuable time another way.

A Place for the Lonely

Presenting a relevant message is a welcome challenge. We are forced to pare down our list of core beliefs to the bare minimum. In a postmodern culture, our set of non-negotiables better be tight, purposeful and, especially, relevant. A few years ago I read the deed for the church building where I work. This deed was written in 1961 and states that no one is allowed to preach here who holds anything other than an amillennial view. In 1961 the leaders of this congregation made that a non-negotiable faith issue. In the entire decade of the 90s, I have not heard a single message regarding different millennial views and which view we should hold. Millennial issues are not viewed as relevant today and, to be honest, they really make little difference in how we live. God's final judgment is the non-negotiable issue that will make a difference, though. Surely we have something relevant to say about the impact Jesus' return has on our lives.

Moving from one house to another is a real pain but moving also offers some great opportunities. We have the opportunity to sort through all that old stuff we have accumulated over the years and give the heave to those things which are only taking up space. We don't have room for things we will never use again. Our culture is changing. God's church needs to keep pace with these shifts if we are going to remain relevant. We have a great opportunity to sort through our arguments, our strategies, our methodology, our thinking and conclusions, our questions and answers, our core set of beliefs, our traditions. Have we accumulated some views and opinions which will only take up space in this new era? Are any of these possessions relevant for past days but not very useful for the future? Does anything need to be put aside for the move? Or maybe we need to replace some of our past methodology or cherished questions with different methods and questions to remain current with a changing culture. A move provides a great time to make those changes intentionally as we try to furnish our faith for the future.

Change is such a vital part of our culture today that traveling light has become a necessity. We must do the hard work of prayer as we listen to God tell us what to toss, what to keep, what to alter. We must do the hard work of study so we will have sufficient listening skills and a well-equipped spirit of discernment. Even our vocabulary needs to be examined. When I speak to University of Kentucky students I have no choice but to speak in their language. In their week they do not hear or say the words redemption, sanctification, glorification. Not only must the message be relevant, we must speak with words our audience comprehends. This is also true for the songs we sing. One simple reason we are seeing such a flood of new music is that younger people want to sing to God in words they understand and use every day. Traveling light is something Jesus recommended to his disciples—no purse, no bag, no sandals—and maybe a light load of non-negotiable faith issues would make our travels and conversations in this new millennium more effective for God's Kingdom.

Our Community is Relational

A final challenge we face at this important juncture is for our communities of faith to be highly relational. When we plan an event on campus or when our youth ministry is signing students up for a trip, the big question is not, "Where are we going?" Nor is it, "What are we going to do there?" The question which determines whether or not anyone signs up is, "Who else is going?" Relationships are the key to unlock hearts and souls. We want to hear people's stories because then we can get to know the person. When we think about church in this new millennium, we must place a priority on relationships.

Here is a letter written by a 24-year-old man who missed having a relationship with his father. He never gave it to his father but to me instead as a sort of cleansing exercise. Reading these heartfelt and painful words helps to explain the deep need for genuine relationships in his life. His story is not an anomaly but rather a fairly common occurrence.

>Dear Dad,
>When I was a little kid, I remember you being there for me. I remember when you used to take me to my soccer games early Saturday mornings. You'd put your hand on my head while we walked to that black Oldsmobile. And then we'd do what usually only you and I did. We'd get White Castles for

lunch. Those were the best times. And I remember when you and I would go out and buy building materials together at Lowe's. You taught me a lot. I probably bugged you with lots of questions, but you always had answers. And I remember when you and I would work in your woodshop together on piece of furniture. I wanted to be just like you. I remember while you were building something, I sawed, nailed, and tried to make something on my own just like you did. I felt really good and loved when you asked me to hold a piece of wood while you cut it or you'd let me help you sand something. I felt valuable.

I remember these times and I also have to think of a lot of yearnings I have in my heart. I still want to spend time with you. You give me something that nobody else in the whole world can give me. You're my dad and I need you.

I really wish we could have shared some of the things you and your father shared. You hunted, you fished, you probably adventured together. Why didn't you do those things with me? Was I not good enough or man enough or strong enough to do it? Did you look at how bad I was in sports and think, "He can't do this well, so he probably can't do anything else"? I felt rejected. I asked you to take me fishing and the answer was always "Sometime." You didn't even say "No," so I kept hoping it would happen sometime. I remember when we'd take the fishing poles on vacation and I'd hope that we'd go sometime, just you and me, and fish...but we didn't. The only time we did go fishing was with my cousin and uncle and I felt like I didn't know how to do it. I did it anyway though. I remember resenting my cousin because his dad took him fishing and you didn't. He knew how to do it and I didn't. I was jealous of him for that. I probably would have given up all my toys for times like he had with his dad. And I remember when I was there with the fish on my hook. I was crying because I didn't know what to do. My uncle was the one who helped me and told me what to do, not you. Why wouldn't you help me? And you two laughed about it, about me crying, and it was your fault that it happened anyway because you never taught me how to fish and you left me there all by myself.

Dad, I still need you. I still love you. I want to get to know you better. I want to learn about what kind of man you are, where you come from, who you were when you were young. I want to build things with you. I want to hike, fish, and camp with you. And I want us to do all those things together with my son. Nobody can make up for what I didn't get from you. You are my only earthly father and I know there are no substitutions. I want to learn how to be a man and I'm asking God to give me what you haven't. He is the father of us all and I love him.

My friend longs for a mentor who loves him and teaches him and challenges him and who wants to be his friend. He feels he has not received that from his father. Will the longing for that kind of relationship be found in God's church?

I have another friend whose father died when he was fourteen years old. Going to church was not part of his childhood. When he came to UK, he began dating a girl in our campus ministry, and Jesus found an open heart. Soon he became a disciple. He said to me in one of our Bible studies, "You're the only example of a Christian man I've ever known." God is using me to be his mentor and friend. Just last week I asked a group of students meeting at our home on a weeknight why they chose to be there that night. This same young man simply and honestly responded, "This is where my family is tonight, so this is where I want to be."

We have students come to our church near campus from all different kinds of church experience besides Churches of Christ. For some, our worship assembly is alien. To them we seem unexcited and sometimes even unhappy to be worshiping the God who made us and whose Son died for us. But they still come and they do not whine. They come because this is where their friends are. This is where they find someone to eat lunch with or go to a movie with. These students are going to worship where they are welcomed into a community of people their age. They want to experience God's presence with close friends, not in isolation and not just intellectually.

Unchurched young people with postmodern roots feel far removed from the Christian subculture. Our language, our values, our hope—they do not get it. And they are skeptical. They have seen way too many religious shams. As they surf through the cable channels they see the religious performances, the make-up, the (attempted) professionalism, the flood of tears, the unceasing flow of words and the never-ending appeals for money. If they watch these stations, they do it for entertainment, not for transformation. Every single one of them knows about ministers who have preached one message and lived another. They know and they are skeptical. Can we blame them?

Genuine relationships with Christ-followers have always been one of God's tools for building up his Kingdom. I believe relationships are the primary door through which people enter God's family. Younger people, especially, really do not care about your title, your degrees, your status, your salary. They want to know you and they want to know if you care about them. Providing programs at our churches and tossing them a budget will not cut it with these folks. Providing the opportunity to develop real, loving, committed relationships is what will attract them.

Storytelling may again be an avenue to develop relationships. Church leaders could open the doors for Christians to tell their accounts of how God is moving in their lives. Sunday mornings need those kind of stories. Intergenerational gatherings provide great opportunities for stories of faith to be shared, both by the older and the younger believers. Preachers need to become skilled at telling the story of their own life. People will be able to hear what God has to say if we intertwine His message with our own faith stories.

Another way for us to maintain a relational emphasis is for our churches to keep getting smaller as they continue to grow. Small groups with all sorts of flavors will become more and more necessary. The loneliness is best addressed, however, among more intimate groups where struggles and victories and prayer may be shared. I believe people want to develop accountability with someone else. Smaller groups are the only way to accomplish such intimacy. Every single one of us needs at least one Christian friend with whom we are able to share our heart.

We are advertising a community of faith, a community that encourages, challenges, loves, prays, welcomes, dreams and takes care of each other. People will come to check us out because of what our ad promises. But is that what they will find? Or will the shelves be empty? Will they discover genuineness in our hearts or just a lot of pious talk? Will they find open arms or pointing fingers? Will they discover unconditional love? We are the face of Jesus to so many people who know so little about him. Will our expression and our language be as welcoming as Jesus is? If we're to survive and thrive in this era of postmodernism, we have no option but to become experts at genuine relationships, just like Jesus modeled for us.

I am thankful to be alive in the twenty-first century. I am thankful to be part of Christ's body in this century. I am especially grateful to be part of Churches of Christ in this century. Life in Christ right now is exciting. Change is challenging and challenges are what make us grow. I offer these three challenges to us as we move into the future. Let's celebrate the mystery of God. Let's travel light with a relevant message. Let's long to know each other and to be known through life-changing relationships. May we continue to work alongside God as He does His work in the lives of lonely and lost people.

Note

1. Steven Garber, *The Fabric of Faithfulness* (Downer's Grove, IL: InterVarsity, 1996), 59-60.

13

Can an Institutional Church Become a Missional Congregation?

Grady D. King

We are living in a complicated moment. The challenges of ministry and church life have never been greater—or filled with more opportunity. My religious heritage is deeply rooted in the Churches of Christ. Until the moment I see the face of Jesus I will give my heart to loving, challenging and supporting the Churches of Christ, in good times and bad times. This is not to say that I have not struggled with disappointment and, at times, cynicism. Any group that holds itself up as having arrived at being God's people is destined for self-destruction. Our high regard for Scripture coupled with humanity's supposed ability to "get it right" in all areas of doctrine and doing church has been burdensome and driven me to my knees on more than one occasion.

I do believe that the Churches of Christ have something to contribute to the religious community—respect for God's Word, the theological significance of the Lord's supper, immersion into Christ and the desire to be Christians only. However, it is arrogant to assume that God waited until the American Restoration Movement came along to perfect his church and that the "Churches of Christ" are his faithful remnant above all religious people in the world. Of course, this "faithful, right church" posture is not peculiar to us. It existed within Judaism in the first century among the Pharisees, Sadducees, Zealots and Essenes. They all appealed to the same story and Scriptures, justifying their existence and defending the truth. The "be like us" syndrome is not new, but it is still just as arrogant as it was when Jesus encountered it and Paul resisted it. If we can get it perfectly right, then why do we need God's grace? I believe God's Word is the anvil on which doctrine and church life is forged. But devotion, not perfection is the ideal. When all is said and done, we stand before God as a community of faith dependent upon his grace and power for our existence and growth.

As a Bible-based people, the Churches of Christ should meet the cultural and religious challenges of the new millennium with passion, relevance and clarity. Yet in congregation after congregation, polarization over methods, generational preferences, worship styles and leadership squabbles seems insurmountable. The clouds of despair linger over many a congregation. Too often, "if, then" is the dominant response to the challenges of polarized and static congregations. "If" we just had a better preacher, a new song leader, a praise team, new elders, all read from the same Bible or could find a new program, "then" we would really grow. No doubt churches may need some of these changes. However, it is possible to make all these changes and not address the problem. As Anton Chekhov, the Russian playwright reminded his people at the turn of the nineteenth century, "We are trying to find answers to our problems, when we need to be asking, have we even stated the problem correctly?"

Michael D. Warden provides some insight into stating the problem correctly:

> In the last half of the 20th century, the American religious landscape was transformed. Commitment to traditional church structures steadily waned, while at the same time our hunger for spiritual fulfillment inched its way in to the forefront of cultural dialog. For the first time in our history as a nation, the concept of Truth began to lose its status as an independent reality. Instead, Truth became relative dependent upon an individual's

circumstance or perspective. This is a sign of the times...only one among many. The culture is shifting. And many of the established paradigms by which churches have operated for decades can no longer support a populace that is looking for Truth outside the "box" created by our predecessors. By necessity, the 21st-century church is becoming more flexible and organic, adapting and changing to engage the culture that surrounds it.[1]

Even a casual observer of Churches of Christ would conclude that flexible, organic and culturally relevant does not typify the majority of congregations. For some, even considering the question of cultural relevance is unthinkable because it will lead, they believe to compromise, which is tantamount to unfaithfulness. As a result, we keep doing church in the "come, sit, listen and leave models," tweaking the programs, holding the meetings, creating new ministries, all in hope of God blessing us with a dynamic congregation and some growth. We have come to expect minimal results for our faithfulness. To justify our minimal growth and, in many cases, stagnant church life, we reason that it is a tough world and people are just not very interested in truth.

If this scenario sounds familiar, then you know the frustration of established institutional church life in a postmodern culture. Most of us know the reality of efficient ineffectiveness. Someone has said that insanity is doing the same things over and over and expecting different results. For the law of any system, whether marriage, family, school or church is: "If we always do what we have always done we will always get what we have always got." We must be willing to ask the hard questions and struggle with the implications. Here are a few of those hard questions that lurk in the shadows of every congregation in some way. Who are we? Why are we here? What is happening in our community? How does the community perceive us? What is God calling us to be? What does it mean to be faithful to God, the Gospel and people? If our congregation were to cease to exist tomorrow, would it make any difference at all in our community?

This is the challenge of leadership—to struggle with such questions and foster dialog in the church. Leaders must deal with congregational morale, and nothing helps morale more than leaders who prayerfully engage the church with a Gospel-focused vision. We do not have a choice, if we are to be faithful to God and his redemptive purpose in the world. Every generation fleshes out church and faith in its own way. However, it is human nature to resist change. So we keep thinking and doing the same things expecting different results. Historically, our primary response to the culture, both secular and religious has been one of antagonism and or isolation. We should heed Paul's admonition to watch our life and doctrine closely (1 Tim. 4:16). However, Paul's concern focused on the Gospel message being passed on and the character of the messenger passing it on. Paul's letters to Timothy and Titus were culturally relevant and practically focused. Never did Paul write abstract doctrine removed from the life of the church in the culture. For Paul, a static form of religion was not only unacceptable but lifeless. Paul adamantly opposed "holding to a form of religion, but denying its power" (2 Tim. 3:5). Whether Paul was in urban Ephesus, the villages of Crete or the house churches of metropolitan Rome, the message of the Gospel and the life of the church was indispensable to the growth of the Kingdom.

The church is the presence of God in the world, animated by the Spirit and redemptive in purpose. As God's people, we must be an adaptable, culturally relevant, dynamic, living organism—the body of Christ.[2] Is this how you would describe your congregation? Can this be a reality? Or are we destined to circling the institutional wagons? Will we face cultural and congregational realities with bold, prayerful Kingdom vision and intentional congregational life? Consider the following metaphor as descriptive of the dilemma facing us if we do not struggle with the hard questions.

I grew up going to the Saturday afternoon matinee. A staple of the matinee was the Cowboy and Indian movie. The plot was the same each week: "survive Indian Territory." It was the perennial good versus bad scenario. Indians were portrayed as uncivilized, ruthless savages. Even as a child I knew this portrayal of the American Indian was unjust and historically biased. But it was good entertainment. One of the familiar scenes in almost every movie was the wagon train crossing Indian Territory. When nightfall came, the wagons would circle up in a tight community. It was a safe haven with the campfire at the hub of community life. Around the campfire was good grub, fresh coffee, storytellin', fiddlin' and dancin'. Meanwhile on a nearby plateau the Indians were gathered around a campfire to the sound of war drums and dancing of another sort. Of course, the "White Man" community was oblivious to impending danger, which brings us to the other reason the wagon train would circle up—when Indians attacked. Sometimes the Calvary would arrive just in time, and other times they did not. Though the settlers tried to defend themselves down to the last man, they were outnumbered and strategically disadvantaged. In short, they were unprepared for the territory and circling the wagons was their only option.

So goes the church. We are traveling through "postmodern territory" where the landscape is foreign and the institutional wagon train is becoming more and more obsolete. We continue to circle the wagons around existing forms of being and doing church. For the most part, we gather around the campfire, eat the grub of fellowship and tell stories. Naturally, there is no fiddle playin' or dancin,' and storytelling is limited to a few wagon masters opening up the book on Sunday mornings. There is a whole lot of coming, sitting, listening and leaving until the next time we circle the wagons. It is not all bad and has served us well over the years. However, it is primarily a "come structure" with very predictable events and participation. That is, everything revolves around what we do at the church building—programs, events, worship, sermons, etc. Most established congregations are socially saturated and difficult to get into. We are structured for maintenance, not mission. And it takes a lot of energy and the right stuff to keep the institutional wagon train together and rolling.

Institutionalism is not easy to define. In short, it is a set of attitudes, forms and structures that govern and sustain the institution. When push comes to shove, the existence of the institution becomes more important than any one person or group of people. Whether institutionalism has negative or positive connotations depends upon one's personal needs, core values and experience within institutions. Core values are those things an individual or a group deem important and that function to shape identity. For example, if a congregation values everyone being together in one assembly, then going to multiple assemblies or advocating small groups will be met with great resistance. A congregation will always act consistently with its core values. Any proposed changes reflecting different values are either squelched or left to struggle with little or no leadership support. Without leadership support, they are destined to fail.

The simple fact is that institutions cannot be avoided. Forms and structures must exist. The question is not whether we have them but whether they are effective in enabling us to be the church in any given community. The majority of our leadership discussions focus on whether or not to change the forms, rather than considering whether the forms help us function as the Body of Christ. There is a difference between form and function. The relationship and confusion between form and function lies at the heart of much stagnation in the Churches of Christ. Tim Woodroof, in his book, *The Church That Flies,* explains the difference.

> By "form" I mean those methods, behaviors, and rituals through which the people of God give expression to their life under God—the means they use to carry out the spiritual business to which God has called them. By "function" I intend to denote the spiritual business itself—those ends that are definitional, fundamental, and central to our identity as God people. "Function" addresses mission; "form" addresses the means by which purpose is accomplished. "Function" asks what; "form" asks how. But to say that forms are necessary to function is not to say they are synonymous. The distinction between forms and functions in religious life, between the means of doing business and the essential business itself, is an important one."[3]

Can an Institutional Church Become a Missional Congregation?

The biblical language describing the church as the Body of Christ, family of God and priesthood of believers relates to identity and function. The forms for living out this identity were varied, depending upon the circumstance (i.e., persecution, house churches, etc.).

The relational dynamic of the first-century church cannot be overstated. Even a casual reading of Acts or any of the letters of Paul reveals relational concerns in how they functioned as a church. Unity was certainly not dependent upon uniformity. The Church of Christ was not a religious label over a door but a description of who they were. Our label, "The Churches of Christ" can be problematic. The very phrase "Church of Christ" was never intended by God or used in Scripture as an institutional, static slogan; rather it pointed to a dynamic reality— "the church that belongs to Jesus Christ." This is particularly true in the first century, when most of the congregations were "house churches." Organic, flexible and culturally relevant were marks of the first-century church. They had no choice. The church was passionate about being God's redemptive people.

The first-century church did not exist in a cultural vacuum and neither does the twenty-first century church. This being the case, will congregations of Churches of Christ continue to "circle the wagons" defending our set of institutional forms for doing church? Or will we seek to intentionalize the institution, engaging the culture with the Gospel lived out in relevant and functional congregational life? The world will be the world—we can expect it. But will the church be the church? The problem is not the gospel, nor the church as the manifold wisdom of God (Eph. 3:10). The problem is holding on to an institution to the neglect of God's core value, the church as God's redemptive people.

Simply maintaining certain traditional programs, opening up the church doors for worship, hosting special events, doing community service or supporting missionaries around the world will not sustain us, much less be effective in reaching people. I know. I am preaching in a church I just described. We are a solid, Bible-based, institutional church filled with good people wanting to make a difference. We have a long history of supporting missionaries. However, the challenge before us is not just to support missionaries but become a missionary congregation. We have a vision statement and are struggling to develop strategic mission initiatives to fulfill the vision. On top of all this, we are striving to be a cross-cultural church. 76 language groups are represented in the school district of 30,000. Down at church, however, we are 95% anglo-middle class. To be a missional church we must consider the culture around us. We have made a choice to stay in our present location and we realize, for the most part, that business as usual will not even begin to move us in a missional direction. We are backed into a corner, dependent upon God working among us. Church must become a life we participate in rather than just an event we attend.

Like most churches, we are overloaded with events and activities centered on the church building. Is it bad? No? Is it incomplete? Most definitely. It is more comfortable to "come to church" as a spectator than participate in the church as a community of faith. Most church members have accepted a model of church that is event-centered and building-oriented. Should we be surprised? We have taught our people to come, sit, listen and leave. But they leave as spectators making judgments on the event, rather than participants in the life of God. Coming to an event allows individual freedom without commitment to anyone.

Individualism is seductive and makes religion a private rather than communal experience. This is unhealthy because it is inconsistent with God's nature and what it means to be his people in the world. God is relational. From Genesis to Revelation, the message is the same—God relating, redeeming and renewing the people created in his image. Among other things, being made in God's image means we are relational creatures. The forms of church must facilitate relational intentionality and accountability. If we do not function relationally, we minimize God's power in and through us.

What are we to do? It is not feasible, nor possible to discard one's congregational history or institutional life and start over. However, some key principles cannot be ignored if we are to be a missional people.

Can an Institutional Church Become a Missional Congregation?

1. Think like missionaries.

We live today in the Acts 17 world of Athens rather than the Acts 2 world of Jerusalem. What can we assume about the people in Acts 2? Certainly they were Jews. And being Jews, they would be monotheistic—believing in the one God. They would have knowledge of the Torah (the Law of God) and know something about the promised Messiah. Peter's sermon reflects their understanding. In contrast, Paul addresses an audience in Acts 17 rooted in paganism, mystery religions, Greek philosophy and idols. In short, a pluralistic religious culture. How we preach, teach and relate to those in Jerusalem and Athens is radically different.

Entering the new millennium demands serious reflection about what it means to live in Athens and not Jerusalem. No longer can we assume that American society as a whole is sympathetic to Judeo-Christian values, or that there is a moral consensus woven into the fabric of the American way of life. Religion in America is political, individualistic, self-absorbed and divorced from personal ethics. Interest in spirituality is high, but it is not necessarily a biblical spirituality focused on Jesus as the Son of God and Savior of the world. To think like missionaries means we seek to understand the culture, speak the language, build trust, and sow the seed of the Kingdom through genuine relationships of care and service. Missionaries are "go" rather than "come" oriented. They are flexible in method, gospel-driven and dependent upon God opening up doors. They invest themselves in people, and prayer is indispensable to their existence. Prayer is God's greatest kingdom resource. Effective missionaries are not soloists, but team players modeling community life and utilizing each others gifts. Church is participatory in nature and a haven of hope, not an obstacle course designed to disqualify believers.

Until we begin to see ourselves as missionaries, we will not begin to act in missional ways. First, missional thinking begins with prayer and openness to God's Word. Utilize your present structure of Bible classes to study God's missional nature—his heart, character and redemptive behavior. Second, establish a local mission team to study your community—demographics, trends and school system challenges.

Meet with community leaders and listen closely. Identify community needs that your congregation can address. Keep in mind that building relationships is the focus, not running programs. In fact, most cities have lots of programs already in place needing volunteers. Are you willing to let go of controlling programs in your building and utilize the community resources for the sake of fostering relationships? Remember, missional churches are "go" not just "come" oriented.

2. Develop a congregational vision.

Vision is the North Star of a congregation. It describes who you are and want to be. It is more than words for a bulletin masthead or a church slogan. "Vision cannot become a reality if it is not shared. A vision is shared when individual members of the congregation hold a similar image, and aspire together to achieve the future suggested by the image."[4] Vision is the responsibility of leadership. It is not promoting a cause, but cultivating an atmosphere of God's work in and among his people and the world. If the vision is to make a difference in the life of the congregation, there must be congregational participation in forming the vision.

Here is our vision: "To the glory of God and by the power of the Holy Spirit, we will live the selfless love of Christ in the church and the world." This vision was the product of several months of formal and informal meetings within the congregation and discussion with the leadership. It was at a leadership retreat that we began to do the hard work of processing our congregational history, community issues, key passages and concepts as well as lots of prayer and dialog about what God was already doing in our congregation. The vision helps make decisions for us. It guides us regarding ministries, preaching, worship, ethics and outreach. We state it often publicly and it is even prayed in elders meetings. It is the long-term picture of who we want to be.

Living out of vision, rather than institutional maintenance clarifies leadership. A word of caution—if it takes the leadership one month to process, it will take the church one year. This one month/one year rule is not encouraging for those wanting immediate change. I fought this rule for years, but have come to know just how true it is, mostly because of frustration and failure. Of course, it always depends on the nature of the change. Transitioning an institutionally-based congregation to a missional church is a long-term process.

3. Leaders must lead.

There is a significant difference between leadership and management. Management is most often concerned with efficiency and maintenance. Leadership is concerned with effectiveness and mission. Although leadership and management are not mutually exclusive, the dominant posture of leaders in established institutions generally defaults to management. This underscores the need for vision. Yet vision without pastoral care is unhealthy. Pastoral care is the spiritual feeding and caring of others. It is helping others grow in Christ through encouragement, admonishment, prayer and study. The essence of it is the practice of the one-anothering passages. Regardless of the size of the congregation, it is unreasonable and impractical for the elders to do all the pastoral care and keep the vision alive. De-centralizing pastoral care in light of the congregational vision can be facilitated through creating relational structures.

4. Create functional, relational structures.

The larger a church becomes the smaller it must become. From 1994 to1996 the German Institute for Church Development conducted the most thorough study to date of the causes for church growth. 1000 churches in 42 countries and 5 continents were part of the study. The study resulted in Christian Schwarz's work, *Natural Church Development: A Guide to Eight Essential Qualities of Healthy Churches.* The eight essential elements are: empowering leadership, gift-oriented ministry, passionate spirituality, functional structures, inspiring worship service, holistic small groups, need-oriented evangelism and loving relationships. These elements are defined and explained as principles, not specific methods particular to any one tradition or doctrinal orientation. The work is grounded biblically and theologically. All eight areas are essential and weak areas cannot be ignored; but Schwarz states, "If we were to identify any one principle as 'most important,' then without a doubt it would be the multiplication of small groups."5

People are hungry for spiritual community. Institutional churches given to holding events where members come, sit, listen and leave will become increasingly ineffective in a postmodern world. The postmodern person is seeking authentic relationships, a sense of belonging, and more importantly, a place to participate in and experience religion. Groups that only exist for themselves or get together to "meet and eat" are not holistic. Holistic groups include study, fellowship, prayer, worship, support and an empty chair for a new person. These groups are essential for assimilation of members, pastoral care and inviting unbelievers. For our congregation, this is one of the greatest challenges we face. To ignore it is to commit congregational suicide. The key is equipping relational leaders with a Kingdom vision. Without leaders who care about people and are proactive in fostering relationships, there will be no growth and little life in the institution.

5. Equip Relational Leaders with Kingdom Vision.

The essence of the Kingdom of God is God's reign in the lives of people. It is practicing the Lordship of Christ in every area of life. This goes beyond church life on Sunday. One of the greatest tragedies of institutional church life is that people can hide. And it is not limited to large churches. There are ways to hide in a small church escaping any sense of community, transparency or accountability. A kingdom vision begins with the call of the gospel in the lives of people. Leaders must face this reality and call others into ministry for the growth of the kingdom rather than asking for volunteers to staff a program. It is God's work.

We often ask, "How are you doing?" when we need to be asking, "How are you doing spiritually?" This focuses the conversation immediately and opens up doors for ministry without exception. Equipping relational leaders involves modeling community life—prayer, study, confession, fellowship and worship. Consistency and accountability are not optional. Leaders must mentor and develop leaders. It is the 2 Timothy 2:2 principle: "Entrust to faithful people who will be able to teach others as well" (*NRSV*). As relational leaders are developed new groups and eventually new churches can be planted. In metropolitan areas, new churches need to reflect their global communities. After all, the culture of the cross is being cross-cultural. Planting new churches was in our DNA at one time in the Churches of Christ.

I have not given up on the institutional church. I believe institutional churches can be healthy, vibrant, God-glorifying and Gospel-driven. But business as usual in the new millennium will not get the job done. There is always a price to pay. We do not grow the church. God does. Our task is to submit to God as his servants and live passionately for Christ. The power is in the Gospel. Scripture does not speak in terms of "us" growing, building or promoting the Kingdom of God. The Kingdom is a reality we receive or enter on God's terms. God does the growing.

The Kingdom of God is not threatened by postmodernism or any other philosophy. After all, when the kingdom is preached and lived out in God-dependent community life, people will receive and enter the Kingdom. God is at work in the Churches of Christ. There is hope from where I stand and preach. To God be the glory for the great things he has done and will do.

Notes

1. Michael D. Warden. "The Missional Church: Being the Church in Today's World" NEXT (2nd Quarter, 2000). Leadership Network. 2500 Cedar Springs Rd., Suite 200, Dallas, TX 75201.

2. For a thorough discussion of the church as an "organism" rather than an "organization," see Christian A. Schwarz, *Natural Church Development (A Guide to Eight Essential Qualities of Healthy Churches)*, 1996. ChurchSmart Resources, 390 East Saint Charles Road, Carol Stream, Illinois, 60188. 1-800-253-4276.

3. Tim Woodroof, *A Church That Flies: A New Call to Restoration in Churches of Christ* (Orange, CA: New Leaf Books, 2000), 39-40. This timely and insightful book provides an indepth treatment of form and function while

judiciously considering implications for the Churches of Christ as a restoration people. It is necessary reading for church leaders.

4. Norman Shawchuck and Roger Heuser, *Leading the Congregation* (Nashville, TN: Abingdon, 1993), 143. I highly recommend this resource for processing congregational vision, spirituality, change and, most importantly, taking care of oneself while serving others.

5. "Holistic small groups are the natural place for Christians to learn to serve others, both inside and outside the group—with their spiritual gifts. The planned multiplication of small groups is made possible through the continual development of leaders as a by-product of the normal group life. The meaning of the term 'discipleship' becomes practical in the context of holistic small groups; the transfer of life, not rote learning of abstract concepts." (*Natural Church Development*, p. 32)

14

A Plea for Passion

Buddy Bell

You could hear it in Jesus' voice. Passion. It wasn't there when they left him, but it was now. Pure. Unadulterated. Passion. He had been tired, weary, and hungry. The disciples dutifully came back with food urging him to "eat something." His reply was very curious, "I have food to eat that you know nothing about." You can imagine their thoughts. Who brought it to him? Did he order out? Was there a drive through in Samaria? Jesus interrupts their wandering thoughts with a bolt of red-hot passion, "My food is to do the will of him who sent me and to finish his work!" To put it in our words, Jesus was fired up!

What had happened? Jesus had connected with a five-time divorcee, now shacked up with a man, and offered her living water. And she had drunk deeply! It was a great moment for Jesus. You could feel his enthusiasm. Think about what Jesus had encountered to this point in the book of John. In chapter one, he calls his first disciples. Great guys, but they don't seem to get it. In chapter two, he goes into the house of God, the temple, and it's been turned into a shopping mall, not a place of worship. In chapter three, Nicodemus, a member of the Jewish ruling council, comes to see Jesus. This religious scholar can't seem to understand what it means to be born again. And now, here in "God-forsaken" Samaria Jesus talks to a woman who seems to understand. The message connects. Her life begins to change. And Jesus is pumped!

This proved to be a teachable moment for his disciples then and I pray it can be for us today. We desperately need passion like Jesus. In Churches of Christ today we are known for many things, but passion is not one of them. The problem seems more acute than ever. A movement that once had a clear self-identity and undeniable passion finds that identity questioned and its passion waning. Many of us can remember the excitement we felt years ago when it was reported that the Church of Christ was the fastest growing religious group in America. Members passionately "canvassed" their neighborhoods setting up "cottage meetings" using high tech equipment (film strip projectors) to show "colorized" film strips to our religious neighbors. We were right. They were wrong. We knew it. And we were excited.

It has been a long time since I have seen that kind of passion among our people. In fact, our movement has so emphasized the intellectual that we looked at anyone with passion with a suspicious eye. It was never actually said, but it was certainly understood when I was growing up that we were not to get too excited about Jesus. That was what "the denominations" did. I was struck at a young age by how effective that message had been. I vividly remember all the Sunday night services I attended when the crowd was small and scattered and some good brother would approach the microphone and say, "Our attendance is low tonight and we are scattered, so let's all move down front. It will improve our singing." You would have thought he had asked us to play a piano! Hardly anyone would move. In a really good church, a half a dozen would move. The rest were unmovable no matter how many pleas the brother made. I didn't understand it. I still don't. I once commented in a sermon, "the early church was so excited about Jesus, they went into all the world. We would be down right thrilled if some of you would just move up a couple of pews."

I have wondered all my preaching life what it would take to have it again? I for one am unwilling to go back to a sectarian, arrogant outlook and message. Even those among us who still subscribe to such a message don't seem to have such passion.

I have tried a few different approaches in my preaching in an attempt to elicit such passion. I have quoted Romans 12:11 to the church, "Never be lacking in spiritual zeal, but keep your spiritual fervor, serving the Lord." I would follow the passage saying, "Don't you realize you have been commanded to be fired up, so be fired up!" Needless to say, that approach didn't work. After many years, I found another approach that was much more successful. I would come before the church and make statements like this, "Either you get fired up now, or you will later." It would stir up passion, but it wouldn't last. This kind of fearful approach worked for about three weeks. Then the guilt trip would end and so did the passion.

What would it take for us to have the passion of Jesus who said, "My food is to do the will of him who sent me and to finish his work"? For his food to be my food? I think the answer lies in the next verse. Jesus then looked at his disciples and said, "Do not say, 'Four months more and then the harvest.' I tell you open your eyes and look at the fields! They are ripe for harvest." The key to Jesus' passion was Jesus' vision! He was passionate because he had a vision of the way things were supposed to be. He didn't just see a sinful woman, he saw someone God loved. He didn't see a crowd of half-breed Samaritans, he saw a harvest of souls.

Again, the key to his passion was his vision. This was even true when Jesus went to the cross. How could he voluntarily choose the way of the cross? According to Hebrews 12:2, Jesus was able to "endure the cross" because he had a picture in his mind of the "joy set before him." He could live through the pain and torture of the cross because he could see what it would mean for us. His vision fed his passion.

I am afraid that the reason we don't have much passion is because we don't have much vision. It is vision that feeds passion. You can't work yourself up into some kind of passion. You can't command it. You can't be guilt-tripped into it. You must have a vision big enough, Godly enough, and clear enough, to ignite your passion.

If you are content with the status quo, why get fired up? Keeping things the way they are is not enough to ignite our passion. At this point in the history of our movement, what is most bothersome is not that we have problems or that we face many challenges, but that so many of us seem to be content with the way things are. I ask, "Where are the dreamers among us?"

For too long we have settled for a sub-scriptural vision. We have settled for routine emotionless worship assemblies that don't match the fervor of the early church. We have settled for superficial relationships that don't compare to the depth of love found among early Christians. We have settled for little evangelism in our churches, when the first-century church witnessed people becoming Christians daily. We have settled for little evidence of the power of God in our lives unlike what happened in the book of Acts. We have been satisfied with less than what would please God.

Too often my vision has been limited by my experience. In other words, the best congregation I've ever been a part of will become my vision for what the church should be like. Anything beyond that seems unattainable or suspect. Let's not let our experience be our standard, but God's dream for the church revealed in scripture. Truly this is true to the plea we have made among the religious world for two centuries. As Jesus said, we must "lift up our eyes." We need to walk into our assemblies, our classes, our homes and our communities and have the courage to ask, "What would God have happen here? If God could have his way here, what would he do?" I like what George Bernard Shaw said, "Some people see things as they are and ask, Why? I see things as they are not and ask, Why not?" We need humble, God-loving, Bible-believing Christians today to ask, "Why not?"

One person defined vision "as the ability to sense God's presence, to perceive God's power, and to focus on God's plan in spite of circumstances." Everything changes when you put God in the picture. We must do more than come up with our own plans achieved by our own power. That will only lead to frustration, not passion. If it is not from God it is not worthy of our devotion or capable of igniting our deepest passion.

A Plea for Passion

Let's not settle for anything less than God's vision for us. We cannot settle for traditions of the past that are less than God's vision. On the other side, let's not settle for a new tradition whose greatest hallmark seems to be a rejection of the old ways. In many quarters one form of arrogance has been traded for another form of arrogance. Both come up empty, unworthy of our devotion and incapable of igniting our passion.

It all starts with a vision of God. In Isaiah 6 God's people were in much the same position we are in as a movement today. Things were changing and changing quickly. King Uzziah had passed away. He had been king for 52 years. Superficially he had been very effective, but inwardly the nation had grown corrupt and passionless for God. The nation was affluent and religious but spiritually dead. Though this was true, the people had found a great deal of security in the old ways and were frightened by the future. What was needed was an encounter with God. Isaiah sees the Lord. His reaction is not "Wow!" like we might expect, but "Woe!" He is humbled and feels unworthy to be in God's presence. God sends an angel with a hot coal from the altar to cleanse Isaiah. He has not only encountered the holiness of God, but also his grace! When he hears God's voice saying, "Whom shall I send? And who shall go for us?" he responds, "Here am I. Send me!" (6:8). Just a couple of verses before this he feels unworthy to even speak, now he wants to be God's spokesman. What happened? He encountered God! He leaves on fire for God!

Today the passion of our movement has grown cold. The winds of change are blowing. The security of the old ways is being ripped away. Many are frightened by the future. We need an encounter with God! We need to experience his holiness and his grace. This best takes place in worship. The focus of worship must be more than routine "acts" or the latest change; it must be God. Our way of determining what has been a good worship assembly must go beyond our likes and dislikes; we must ask, Did I encounter God? Both privately and corporately we must continue to seek the face of God. We must fall on our face in humility before the awesome holiness of God and we must be uplifted by his amazing grace. When this happens, we will respond to the call of God with the passion of Isaiah, "Here am I. Send me!"

Not only will this kind of encounter revive our passion, it will change us. Paul describes it this way: "we, who with unveiled faces all behold the Lord's glory, are being transformed into his likeness with ever-increasing glory, which comes from the Lord, who is the Spirit" (2 Cor. 3:18). It is a basic principle of life that you become like what you focus on. We've all experienced having a best friend and picking up on their mannerisms and attitudes. You find yourself saying what they would say and thinking like them. You don't have to work at it, it just naturally occurs. Some studies even say that when a husband and wife are married over a long period of time, they begin to look alike. I know I've just frightened all the wives, but the principle is true. You become like what you focus on. That is why worship is not only commanded, it is necessary if we are to be transformed into the image of Jesus Christ.

For too long our focus has been on issues and not on Jesus. This is true in many traditional congregations where almost any Sunday you attend you'll hear a message on one of our "distinctive marks," but hardly ever hear a message on the cross. Surprisingly, this is true in many of our "non-traditional" churches where you might here a different slant on the same issues, but nonetheless still a focus on issues. We must restore the spirit of the Apostle Paul who said, "I determined to know nothing among you except Jesus Christ and him crucified" (1 Cor. 2:2). Wouldn't that be a true biblical "distinctive mark"?

As we catch a vision of God, we will also begin to catch a vision of his mission for us. The scriptures will reveal to us the dream that God has for his people. We must raise the question consistently; "What would God have happen here?" In other words, if God could have his way in my life or the life of the church, what would he do? We need to encourage our people to re-dream the dream!

The dream of a couple of generations ago has lost the power to transform us and motivate us. Robert Dale discusses this in his book, *To Dream Again*. He writes that when a church moves beyond ministry to nostalgia, questioning and polarization, it is in grave danger.

A Plea for Passion

Certainly we are honest enough to see all three of these in our movement. He goes on to assert that the way to revitalize a church is to go back and dream again. Many of us have never had this privilege and therefore do not have the enthusiasm of those who did it generations before us.

Let's reopen the word of God to catch his vision. Let's fall on our knees and ask for his vision. And let's make ourselves available to accomplish his will. We must go beyond all the polarization and conflict to ask, "What is the heart of God? What is he really concerned about? What were the 'big deals' in scripture? What would it mean in my community for 'his kingdom to come, his will to be done on earth as it is in heaven'?"

This openness to search God's word marked the beginning of our movement and lit a fire that blazed across this country. We've made mistakes. We've drifted from the central focus. Let's learn from our mistakes, but let's not give up on our plea.

I know of a congregation that has experienced this. From every measurable viewpoint the church was in decline. The elders were cornered after every service with complaints. They were attacked by the "right wing" and the "left wing." People were leaving. No one enjoyed "church." Very few were being saved. Finally at a critical point with three elders left, they decided enough was enough. They were tired of seeking to please men and decided to seek to please God alone. They got on their knees and asked God to reveal his plan. They called the church to a higher mission, to reach their community. They hired a staff to implement a plan to carry out the mission. The critical question being asked was not, "Is it traditional or non-traditional, but is it biblical and is it effective?"

This had been in the past a very proud, traditional church. The kind of place where women were required to wear dresses and coffee in a Sunday School class was a major source of contention. When the change began, so did the attack. The elders were threatened to either fire the new minister or have the church torn apart. When they wouldn't fire the preacher, letters warning of the church's apostasy were sent to every family. The next Sunday the leadership went before the church to mark the brother making the threats and to respond to each charge and to share their vision of a church committed to Scripture, focused on Jesus, intent on reaching the lost, but unbound by tradition. The church was called to a vision bigger than themselves. They were called to stretch and even be uncomfortable in order to see God's mission accomplished.

What happened? A few families left (many fewer than anyone anticipated). A spirit of unity and freedom enveloped the church. Worship assemblies began to be a place of diverse worship styles focused on one God. A message of God's grace was exalted. People began to openly confess their sins and pray for one another. Brotherhood issues were discussed in love but never allowed to dominate. Members began to invite their friends. They came and many were saved. Those who were the most frightened by the changes began to be excited about what God was doing. The church exploded with growth. In four years it grew from an attendance of a little over 300 to over 800. A great vision led to great passion and unity! God was glorified.

As Churches of Christ listen for God's call in this new millennium, let's remember...

1. *We live in a negative, cynical world.* This should not come as a surprise to us. If I didn't know Jesus, I would be negative and cynical. Wouldn't you? Often Christians seem shocked that sinners act like sinners! In our culture it is in vogue to be negative. A teenager in a school lunch room can't brag on the food no matter how good it is. How many daytime talk shows would win ratings war if normal people who are positive about life were interviewed? The problem is when the church becomes as negative and cynical as the world.

2. *God has called us to be different, to be holy.* In the midst of a negative and cynical world we should stand out as a positive force for God. How will people see this? Jesus put it in the simplest of terms, "By this shall all men know that you are my disciples, that you love one another as I have loved you." Paul said it was through the church that "the manifold wisdom of God would be displayed...." In the first century this was displayed by the fact that Jews and Gentiles, men and women, even slaves and masters would meet together in unity in the

name of Jesus. In every century the same as been true, our love for one another is what makes us different.

3. *God has called us to make a difference.* We don't live in some kind of isolated dream world. We know better than anyone how bad things are. However, there is one big difference—we see God! That changes everything. We believe that he has the power to use us to make a difference. To be salt, that unseen yet powerful presence that makes life on this earth better. To be light, that open testimony to God's grace that brings him glory.

4. *God's work in our fellowship will be limited by the size of our vision.* What we are really discussing is faith. Do we believe that God can do "immeasurably more than we ask or imagine according to his power that is at work within us"? When Walt Disney World in Orlando was opened in 1974, Mrs. Disney was sitting by Walter Cronkite. Walt Disney had passed away a few years before this. Walter Cronkite wanted to say just the right thing to Mrs. Disney, so finally he leaned over to her and said, "Wouldn't it be great if Walt were here to see this today?" Mrs. Disney wisely replied, "If Walt had not first seen this, you would not see it today!" He saw it before it ever happened. Certainly, this is true by faith. Nothing will be accomplished that we first don't see by faith. If you were God, would you choose to work among and through a group of people who were not sure if you would still work today, who had no expectation of your intervention? Let's not limit God's work among us by our lack of vision.

5. *The closer I grow to God the greater my vision.* Jesus makes it plain throughout the gospels that he has the Father's vision. He was so close to his father that they had the same dream for humanity. The same is true for us. If we want a great vision, we must grow close to God. Any vision won't do. Let's walk with Jesus through the gospels and look at life through his eyes. Let's read Scripture looking for the heart of God. We can't help but pick up on his vision for our world.

6. *A great vision will lead to great passion.* Our lack of passion as a movement is a direct indictment of our lack of vision. When we begin to see God's vision, when we begin to see things the way they are supposed to be, we will have the passion of Jesus. We will no longer have

to be begged to sacrifice for the cause. Some days we might even skip a meal and say, "My food is to do the will of him who sent me and to finish his work." What fills us up, sustains us, fires us up, is to be a part of His work! Some will begin to raise the voice of concern saying, "Let's be careful, let's not get too excited." How long will we fall to this kind of scare tactic? We don't have this problem. I would love to see us have to calm someone down! But, until we have to do that, let's deal with a problem we do have, a lack of passion. Won't it be great when we are known as the people with the greatest passion for God!

I am always amazed looking in the book of John at who catches Jesus' vision first. It's not Nicodemus. It's not the apostles. It's not the priest in the temple. It's not his own flesh and blood. It is the most unlikely person—a Samaritan woman. John writes, "Many of the Samaritans from that town believed in him because of the woman's testimony....They said to the woman, 'We no longer believe just because of what you said; now we have heard for ourselves and we know that this man really is the Savior of the world" (John 4:42). What an amazing thought: this woman becomes the first Christian missionary. This woman who came to the well in the middle of the day in order to avoid the condemning stares of the people, shares her testimony with the entire city. This five-times-divorced, immoral woman turns her world upside down and toward Jesus.

If God could use this woman, please explain why God couldn't use us? At this point in history we may not look like the most likely candidate, but neither did she! Let's catch His vision, get busy on His mission, through the strength of His passion! Pure. Unadulterated. Passion.

Conclusion

A Dream Worth Keeping

Lynn Anderson

In the opening lines of this book Leonard Allen shoves our minds out into the unnerving turbulence of postmodern culture where we may tumble for decades.

Some say this worldview began with European existential philosophers. Some blame Einstein's theory of relativity for the first crack in our foundations. Others trace postmodernism to the counter-culture of the 1960s.[1] Still others say old thought categories fell with the Berlin wall.

Some see democracy as an accessory after the fact. At first democracy meant: one person, one vote. Now it means: don't ask God about right and wrong, ask George Gallup. 'The voice of the people is the voice of God." Pluralism figures in too. When Lady Liberty beckoned the "huddled masses," she gathered a rainbow of worldviews each bringing its own take on truth.

Then when science and the humanities failed to solve complex problems, mistrust of rational thought and human potential became widespread. Rationalism is, for significant masses, outdated. Images, intuition and imaging now move people more than logical, linear reasoning. Our day doubts there is any "True Truth." Things are relative at best. Thus, since there are no absolutes in morals or ethics, "what is right for you may not be right for me."

At least two more spices flavor this brew: pragmatism and immediacy. Forget core values or the common good or the long-term implications. Do what "works for me"—now.

If this new world has any supreme value it is tolerance. It is tolerant of anything but intolerance. Even tolerant of Christianity—but not of "exclusive" Christians. Christian evangelism is therefore "intolerance."

In yesterday's world the person best informed on truth and absolutes was an "authority figure." But where there is no "true truth" of course there can be no Authority Figures. So now we are devoid of heroes. Some even revere anti-heroes. Witness crowds drawn by Madonna, Snoop Doggy Dog, Dennis Rodman or Eminem.

Many in today's world know that yesterday's "brain trust" failed to improve their world. "In fact, those 'smart' boomers busted our world. Education is busted. Family is busted. Sex is busted. Trust is busted. World peace is busted. Marriage is busted. Health care is busted. Government is busted. Even the Supreme Court. It's all busted."

Consequently the new postmodern generation tends toward profound pessimism. Contrast Woodstock in the 1960s with Woodstock in the 1990s. In the 60s thousands of young people "orgied" in a muddy pasture and sang about changing the world. In the 90s thousands of young people "orgied" in the same muddy pasture and sang songs of hopelessness. "The boomers are still in control. We are powerless to change things. So let's grab what we can get from the moment."

Trust has all but vanished too. You can't trust the coach. Nor the principal. The cop is likely crooked. Even the superior courts have become political. The president philanders and lies. The election is suspect. Even my parents didn't keep their promises to each other. Who can we trust? So these times find growing numbers of kids feeling ever more alienated.

This is a world of endless hours of powerful but vacuous and fragmented media. It reads less and less. Thus our time is losing its sense of soul, inwardness and depth. It is a world adrift.

Of course, as Ford says, the "concept of a single generation with a single mindset is only a convenient shorthand grouping of a number of complex sociological dynamics."[2] These groupings are national statistical abstracts, not necessarily any real persons. Nevertheless, a new world has come which is often "angry, alienated and depressed; they are pessimistic, yet accelerating into a frightening future at warp speed. They are in crisis, obsessed with death and suicide prone. Distrustful of authority and wary of the system. They cannot conceive of 'true truth.' Their past is full of pain, and their future is a brick wall. They see the world as user-unfriendly, overcomplicated, chaotic and unstructured."[3]

Overstated? Possibly. True of everyone? Of course not. Yet this sketch touches the tempo of our times, leaving some Christian leaders feeling out of control in a whitewater canyon of flux and chaos.

Can Christians Flourish in Times Like These?

Let me say emphatically that these are not days for Christians to huddle in fear and bash the culture. This generation is not the enemy. "The Christian pilgrim," as Paul Ramsey said many years ago, "should pass from one age to another with the ease and serenity of freedom, assisting the new which is always struggling to be born, because in every age he loves not the times or some abstract truth but the neighbor."[4] Rather, in spite of the fact that "this is a generation with many needs," thoughtful believers see "each of these needs as an opportunity for God and his Son."[5]

The early church flourished in times like these. Actually, in some significant ways our world looks more like the world of the New Testament than any era between the two. In fact, the Buster worldview may share more biblical values than does the Boomer worldview. And if we keep preparing for the future of the church, these may well turn out to be some of the best years in the history of the faith.

However, the gospel will enter postmodern hearts through new doors. We must rethink how we define, defend and spread faith where rationalism is outdated and where people see no absolute values. Our day calls for persuasion which transcends rationalism. "New" persuasion may need to be more like the "old" persuasion of the New Testament.

First, these times call for *a new apologetic*. My old apologetic is passé. Reason and logic will not easily convince postmodern people toward "absolute truth" or toward faith in Jesus. We do not suggest that a new apologetic should be irrational or anti-rational. Of course the mind must stay in the game. But rational thought is not the only player on the field.

And words carry much less freight in this new world than does an "embodied message." The old saw was never more timely: "I'd rather see a sermon, than hear one any day." For example, Milton Jones says that, "Fifteen years ago we could walk through a university dorm and organize a Bible study any day of the week. That won't work now. But today we can walk through a dorm and recruit a service project team any day of the week."

Second, *story*: Young hearts sing, "tell me the story of Jesus." This is actually not a new approach but a return to a biblical apologetic. The Bible is itself a sweeping story with God at the center. Jesus mostly told stories rather than exegeting texts or positing airtight propositions. And the book of Acts is a story. Even so today, hearts are moved when we authentically tell how The Story intersects with Our Story.

These times also call for *fresh strategies*. "Fresh" however does not necessarily mean "new." Most "strategies" of the first-century church fit the twenty-first century culture. The more biblical the strategy the more effective it may be today.

For example, these times are post-rationalistic. There are more ways of knowing than the "head" way. Today's world has little trouble accepting the supernatural. It has more appetite for the transcendent and for mystery than yesterday's world. The Christian story is of course a story of supernatural events and intervention.

And these times definitely seem post-denominational. Hallelujah! Isn't that what we in the Restoration Movement have always wanted? Here is our opportunity to "re-join" the movement toward non-denominational Christianity, which seems to be going on all around us.

Many postmoderns feel betrayed; the Christian story restores broken trust especially when embodied in people who "will never leave you."

People today often feel vulnerable and insecure; the Christian story brings a sense of protective, healing community in the arms of a loving God.

A Dream Worth Keeping

Many today lack a sense of identity; in the Christian story, identity is clear—Jesus is our identity. "Christ lives in me" (Gal. 2:20).

These days are becoming post-individualistic. Ian Forester in the epigram to *Howard's Inn* tersely captures this longing, "Only Connect." The Christian story is about real community. Not just rhetoric. Nor virtual community. Nor merely finding a group "I feel good in." Rather, real community covenants together on what and whom we are willing to suffer for. This is the Christian story.

Like their first-century counterparts, many people today feel alienated; the Christian Story is about reconciliation. It takes at least two things to communicate the gospel—hearing the word and experiencing the message in real "one another" relationships.

And postmoderns respond to good mentors; they do not believe in Authority Figures. But they seem drawn to Wisdom Figures. Great! Spiritual leaders lead by example, not position, and the Christian story introduces them to a safe and healthy Father and a loving Servant Lord who will be "the same yesterday, today and forever."

We have glimpsed just a few ways the first-century apologetic and strategies can impact the twenty-first century. To summarize: Possibly the best thing the twenty-first century church can do to reach its world is to be the first-century church. Not the medieval church. Not necessarily the Reformation church. Nor the nineteenth-century church. Rather, as Tim Woodruff reminds us, we must recover, not ancient forms, but biblical functions of the early church. We must "take from the altars of the past the fire and not the ashes."

What shall the righteous do when foundations fall? Real foundations never fall! Fifty years ago, at the height of modernism in the western world, pundits proclaimed, "modernism will defeat Christianity." But Christianity is still here, and flourishing, while modernism is dying. Now, some futurists are suggesting, "Christianity won't survive the postmodern period!" But don't you believe it—all the momentum is to the contrary.

Our God is an unchanging God!
Jesus the Christ is "the same yesterday, today and forever!"
The Bible is an unchanging word!

With these eternal foundations and faithful promises we are confident people of hope.

Hopeful Signs

After dinner some months back, a circle of friends sipped coffee and listened politely while I unpacked my mission: encouraging leaders among Churches of Christ. Then Randall, our host, leaned forward and pointedly probed, "Why invest this much energy in Churches of Christ? Hasn't this whole 'restoration' idea proven itself a well-intentioned but failed experiment?" Randal is by no means the only person I've heard ask a question like this.

And, believe me, I understand the questions. While I feel deep emotional attachment to Churches of Christ, still I have considered leavening. At times I despair that we can recover a credible and impacting voice in our world.

However, I have chosen to stay. I must admit that part of the reason I stay is that Churches of Christ are my family, the place of my best memories. But that is not the main reason I have stayed. Nor do I stay because we are "the true church" or "the only Christians." Nor because we are all there is to the Restoration Movement. In fact I believe a great spirit of "Christians only" and "Back to the Bible" is flourishing far outside our diminutive circle.

Why then do I stay? Partly because I have found no answer to the haunting question, "To whom shall I go?" All denominations and non-denominations have their own viruses. So leaving my heritage would not take me away from problems. Besides, I sort of know my way around our place.

However, the central reason I remain deeply committed to Churches of Christ is this: I believe in our movement.

No, I don't endorse all our shibboleths. Or ignore our pathologies. But, in its deepest bosom, our movement still holds an immensely worthwhile ideal, a dream worth awakening among all believers. As Brad Small said to me recently, "The restoration plea is rock solid. When you stand before a group of people and say, 'We will be bound only by the written word of God, as best we understand it. (Not by the silence, but the written word.) And in our faltering way we want to imitate Jesus ministry,' people love that. People from every denomination in town come for that because that's what every believer wants."

Brad should know. His congregation began in 1995 with 34 people. Now average attendance is around 1000. Of the 600 adults (besides hundreds of children) that make up the church, 400 have come to Christ and been baptized there. In fact 158 were baptized in 1999 and 2000.

Ah, yes. Despite our foibles, there is still a lot right with us. True, at times we've appeared dead-ended in a sectarian fortress mentality. Yes, we've sometimes cultured a crippling strain of legalism. But those do not represent the majority of Churches of Christ. And they by no means define our future.

Far to the contrary. I believe we are getting back on mission. Back to the Bible. Back, not to the patterns, but to the principles and power of the early church. And forward to dialogue and partnership with all who seek to follow Jesus and pursue His mission.

I meet monthly with small groups of church leaders across the country—cumulatively now since 1996, 15 groups of 8-12 persons each meeting a full day each month for a year. In the past five years, in larger and less intimate conferences I have interacted with leaders from more than 2,000 congregations. Admittedly this is only a fraction of Churches of Christ, but my sampling says that despite some foibles and flaws there is a lot right with us. A few examples:

Worship Renewal
The critical eye may see only cosmetic touch-ups in our attempts at "worship renewal." Certainly some "renewal" may be only superficial faddishness shaped by "consumer" appetites. But in my experience these are exceptions.

Far more authentic and substantive forces drive the larger worship renewal among Churches of Christ. I see churches hungry for encounter with the majesty and holiness of the Almighty God of sovereign splendor. Hundreds of congregations are inviting God back to the center of the church. I see thoughtfully planned worship in a growing number of churches. More use of the Psalms. More biblical preaching. Thoughtful emphasis on the Lord's Supper. More helpful formats. And many other encouraging signs.

Prayer Renewal
God is also being invited back into the center of daily life-focus as well. Our well-oiled church programs often produce anemic results at best. But there is good news: this frustration is driving us back to God. Only God can change lives and build churches. We are looking to Him with less arrogance and more passion.

Two examples: I recently visited a church where Wednesday evenings are authentic "prayer meetings." At one point, hundreds huddled in circles across the auditorium in prayer. At other moments, people streamed forward to pray with the elders and their wives or to kneel side by side at prayer benches. Many congregations are moving in similar directions. And each group of church leaders with whom I meet monthly spends at least a half hour of every meeting in prayer. Almost everywhere I go I find Christians praying more than ever in my memory.

Grace Message
The biblical grace message is returning to our churches like wild flowers after spring rains. Not that legalism is unique to Churches of Christ. Most fellowships are plagued by their own brands of legalism.

The past decade gave us three key books on grace. Max Lucado's *In the Grip of Grace* was prompted, in part, by legalism in Churches of Christ. But Chuck Swindoll's *The Grace Awakening* and Phillip Yancy's *What's So Amazing About Grace* were prompted by legalism all across Christendom. Legalism seems to be inherent in human fallenness, so that, while the grace message may well have been proclaimed in many churches, our fallen, sinful, religious ears may have been unable—or unwilling—to hear it. Consequently each perceives his or her own heritage as uniquely legalistic. I hear persons of nearly every denomination vent anger at their religious roots.

Nevertheless, we cannot deny our own brand of legalism. Although we spoke the word "grace," some of us still dutifully tried to work our way to heaven. We beat ourselves up for our chronic failure. And we inflicted huge masses of "ungrace" upon one another.

But for at least two decades now, in most of our congregations, we have heard and internalized God's marvelous grace. And as we receive more Grace, we are extending more grace to others. This grace is also inching us out of sectarian isolation into honest, humble interaction with the larger Christian community.

Leadership Renewal
Some time back, several ministers from Churches of Christ spent a day with Lyle Schaller, a respected resource person on church development. We specifically asked him what we "look like from the curb." Schaller said:

> About your polity: You expect your groups of elders to lead in a visionary way. But groups have never been able to lead. Every major move of God was led by a person, not a group. But your congregational polity does not empower "a person" to lead, even though that person may be gifted and trained in leadership. This frustrates everybody—leader and elders. And it dooms your churches to grow no larger than a committee of amateurs can manage, part-time! Most church elders have to work 50-70 hours per week in the market place. So even if they might have the gifts and the expertise for leadership, and even if it were possible for groups to lead, these men simply do not have the time to build flourishing churches.

Ouch and amen!

In our times, however, elders in hundreds of churches are moving away from micro-management, permission withholding/granting and status quo maintaining. They see that "job one" is building persons rather that running organizations. So they are moving toward shepherding, mentoring and equipping. They see that every Christian is a minister. And they are discovering that when members get equipped for ministry, then "each part works properly" and "the body builds itself up in love."

What is more, in church after church, elders are empowering a person—with leadership gifts and training—to lead. This frees up elders to shepherd, and frees up the leader to lead. This huge paradigm shift is of infinitely greater strategic significance than tinkering with "the look" of the assemblies. And churches are finding it both biblical and effective.

Redemptive Community
We are beginning to "Escape from Church Inc." as Glen Wagner would put it, and are returning to real community.[6] Thousands of God-hungry church folks are weary of walking in and then out of large assemblies, without feeling real connection with brothers and sisters in Christ. They long to be the body of Christ again, to experience the church as a family rather than an organization. We are "re-learning" that most life-change happens, not through programs or sermons or seminars—but through authentic relationships. Most people come to Christ that way, grow spiritually that way, and learn ministry skills best that way. Thus the growing interest in small groups, as more and more serious Christians see them as recovery of New Testament *koinonia*, fellowship of the Spirit. Churches across the land are moving this direction.

Missional Churches
From the 60s through the 80s Churches of Christ lost much of their sense of mission. Doubtless multiple factors contributed to this: Backlash against Crossroads/Boston. The inward-focus of the boomer era. Fighting over internal issues. Soul-softening affluence. Cultural pluralism. And antiquated outreach strategies, to name a few.

However, the 90s saw a rising passion for evangelism for many reasons: more effective outreach strategies, inspiration from the evangelistic success the community church movement, revival of spiritual passion in the church generally, to name a few. Here are some signs of this growing sense of evangelistic urgency:

First, a number of our older, larger congregations that had plateaued or begun to decline have experienced amazing turn-arounds. Many churches 25 years old and older are experiencing evangelistic growth far beyond anything from the 60s through the 80s. Some that saw few baptisms for decades have experienced as many as 50, 90, even 200 or more baptisms per year.

Second, we see growing numbers of new church plantings. True, some 80% of new church plantings fail. Some for lack of financing. Some from inadequate leadership. Or ineffective methods. Or because they were born out of protest against the status quo, rather than out a sense of mission. Possibly the most common cause of failed church plantings is that the core people spend too little time nailing down their plan. Then after the "point of no return" they fall into conflict over differing expectations, and the new church either implodes or gridlocks toward slow death.

The good news, however, is that as Chris Smith says (chapter 10) new church plantings are usually much more evangelistically effective than older, more established churches. Not only are we planting more new churches these days, but we are also learning to do thoughtful planning. So I fully expect that church planting success rates will go up, which will in turn spawn more church plantings. Right now many small and not very visible churches are experiencing wonderful evangelistic success. Some churches of 100 to 300 are baptizing as many as 20, 40, 100 persons a year and doing a good job of equipping them for productive ministry. Most important of all, we are measuring evangelism in changed lives and in the growth of healthy churches, not merely in the number of baptisms.

Running Deeper
Possibly the most important trend I see these days is that Churches of Christ are running deeper, not just broader and faster.

Although missional action appears to be on the rise, at the same time we seem less inclined toward mere activism than during some previous eras of evangelistic fervor. I hope this is because we are maturing as a movement. As our theology becomes more biblically balanced, we seem to rely less on human machinations and more on the grace of God. I think we are less impressed with the rewards of our own efforts and more enchanted with God. We seem more drawn these days to wisdom figures of quiet depth than to oratory, academics and accomplishments. We sound less glib in the face of complexity. We are growing more comfortable with ambiguity. And we are learning to stand in wondering awe before *mysterium tremendum*.

A Hopeful Coming Generation
From the start many gifted, well-trained and faithful leaders blessed our movement. But, with all due respect to former generations (after all I am now part of "former generations"), never in our history have we had the number of well-trained, God-impassioned, culturally aware, globally-thinking preachers serving among our churches. The preachers of this generation pray more and unpack the scriptures more skillfully than we did.

Fred Smith, formerly of the interdenominational Leadership Network, once said of the Church of Christ ministers he had met, "These guys are some of the brightest and the best." A few of "the brightest and the best" stand in the limelight pulpits of flagship churches, but a lot more serve effectively in small, out-of-the-way congregations. And armies more are on their way. Enrollment of students headed toward ministry is at an all time high in most of our graduate Bible departments.

However, while the news is mostly good these days, our hope does not lie with emerging leaders. Nor effective elders, nor missional churches, nor effective strategies. Our plea is still valid and overwhelmingly appealing: to be just Christians, guided only by the written word of God, called to imitate the ministry of Jesus. Our hope is in the hands of "the sovereign God of all Hope"—the God who is "new every morning" and "works wonders tomorrow." So, even at our best, we restoration people, we back-to-the-Bible people, are merely tools in the hands of the One who promised, regardless of historical trends or cultural circumstances, "be of good cheer, I have overcome the world."

Notes

1. Gene Edward Veith, *Postmodern Times: A Christian Guide to Contemporary Thought and Culture* (Wheaton, IL: Crossway, 1994), 40-41.

2. Kevin Ford, *Jesus for a New Generation* (Downer's Grove, IL: InterVarsity, 1995).

3. Ibid.

4. Paul Ramsey, *Basic Christian Ethics* (New York: Scribner, 1950), 351.

5. Ibid.

6. Glenn Wagner, *Escape from Church Inc.* (Nashville, TN: Thomas Nelson, 2000).

Bestseller! from New Leaf Books

A CHURCH THAT FLIES
A New Call to Restoration in Churches of Christ
Tim Woodroof

Popular with church leaders who are facing tensions over tradition and change.

"Provides an indepth treatment of form and function while judiciously considering implications for the Churches of Christ as a restoration people. It is necessary reading for church leaders."
—*Grady King*

"In the spirit of informed dialogue, Woodroof's book is well worth reading. Despite much bumpy turbulence, it is certainly the flight of the future on which a newer generation in the church has confirmed reservations." —*F. LaGard Smith*

224 pages, softcover $14.95   Call toll free **1-877-634-6004**

LOOK PRESS

Are you looking for preaching/teaching support as you discuss **A Church That Flies** *with your congregation?*

LOOK PRESS publishes educational materials, including sermon outlines, handouts, small group studies, and even PowerPoint presentations to support your preaching efforts.

Contact us at **1-800-863-5665**

Or log onto our website: www.lookpress.com

We exist to serve you as you serve your church.

A seminal book on *Spirituality* in Churches of Christ

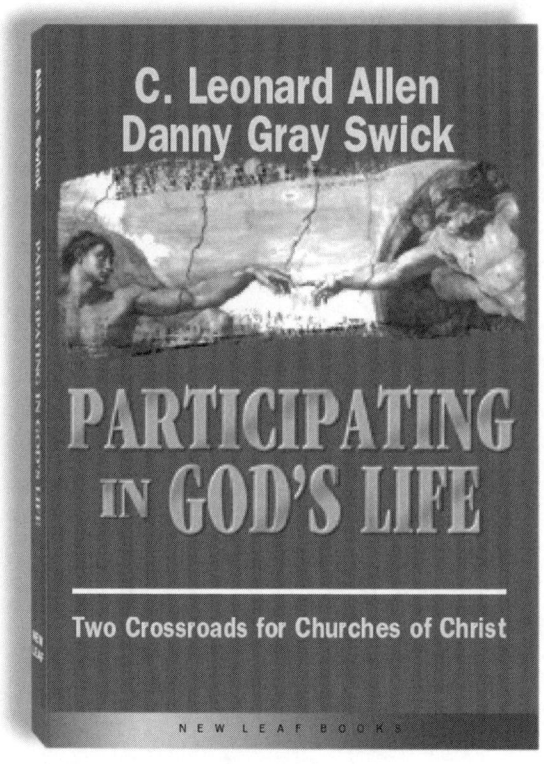

202 pages, paperback $15.95

from the author of
The Cruciform Church
and *Distant Voices*

"Postmoderns yearn for genuine spirituality. Are Churches of Christ prepared to respond to this cultural search? Building on Allen's earlier book, *The Cruciform Church*, this is the first book to robustly explore the meaning of Trinitarian theology for Spirituality in Churches of Christ."

—**JOHN MARK HICKS**,
David Lipscomb
University, Nashville, TN

"The authors, Allen and Swick, address a problem which evangelicals at large face. We have bought into the modern project and lusted after greater rational certainty than we have a right to. As a result, we have also fostered a somewhat Spirit-less kind of religion. This book indicates the way of healing and balance."

—**CLARK PINNOCK**,
Hamilton Divinity College,
Ontario, Canada

To order call toll-free **1-877-634-6004**
or write: NEW LEAF BOOKS, 12542 S. Fairmont, Orange, CA 92869

150 pages, softcover
$11.95

CHRIST—NO MORE, NO LESS
How to be a Christian in a Postmodern World
MIlton Jones, Seattle

"Jones discusses what postmodernism is and how Christians can respond to it. Also provides a study of Colossians as a means of integrating the discussion into a Christian worldview....filled with clear writing, effective illustrations, and pithy nuggets." —*Christian Chronicle (June 2001)*

"I heartily recommend this book to all who want to 'understand the times' so they can share Christ more effectively."
—*Rick Atchley, Richland Hills Church of Christ, Ft. Worth, TX*

148 pages, softcover
$12.95

COMMUNINGS in the SANCTUARY
Robert Richardson

Classic communion meditations delivered in the Bethany Church of Christ in the 1840s and 50s by the biographer of Alexander Campbell.

"To open Communings is to enter a vast, largely unexplored field of 19th century piety. It comes as something of a shock to those who thought they knew their spiritual roots to find a book so completely animated by the love of God and the mystery of God....Taken slowly and meditatively, these masterpieces are sure to awaken the soul to the joys of devotion."
—*Darryl Tippens, Provost, Pepperdine University (in* The Christian Chronicle)

224 pages, paper
$14.95

TRUSTING WOMEN
The Way of Women in Churches of Christ
edited by **Billie Silvey**

Traditionally, most books on women's roles in the church have been written by men. In this volume, a group of women actively involved in various forms of ministry tell their own experiences serving God and his people. These are inspiring stories of faith, struggle and devotion. Excellent for younger women who are seeking God's will for their lives, as well as for older women who are evaluating their life and ministry.

Writers include Lindy Adams, Katie Hays, Anna Griffith, Joyce Hardin, Amy Bost Henegar, Joy McMillan, Lucille Todd, Sherrylee Woodward, Jeanine Varner, Jackie Warmsley, and others.

NEW LEAF BOOKS   **1-877-634-6004** toll free